The Book of Nature

VERMONT LIFE

Book of Nature

RONALD ROOD and Others

INTRODUCTION BY HAL BORLAND

EDITED BY WALTER R. HARD, JR.

THE STEPHEN GREENE PRESS
BRATTLEBORO · VERMONT

ACKNOWLEDGMENTS

The editor and publisher acknowledge indebtedness for use in this book of articles, drawings and photographs which appeared in *Vermont Life* from 1947 to 1967. Particular gratitude is expressed to the Hon. George D. Aiken for permission to quote more extensively from his definitive *Pioneering with Wildflowers;* to Biologist James D. Stewart and Warden Robert J. Mumley of the Vermont Fish and Game Department, whose assistance made the "Gulls of The Four Brothers" article and photography possible in the first place; and to the Vermont Historical Society for the woodcut of the Lake Champlain "sea monster" on page 68. The photographs of ring-bill gulls opposite the title page, of frosted ferns on page viii, of deer tracks in the snow on page xii, and of the late spring orchid on page 81 are by Bullaty-Lomeo. The front-cover photograph is by Hanson Carroll, and the back-cover photograph is by Richard R. Frutchey.

Contents

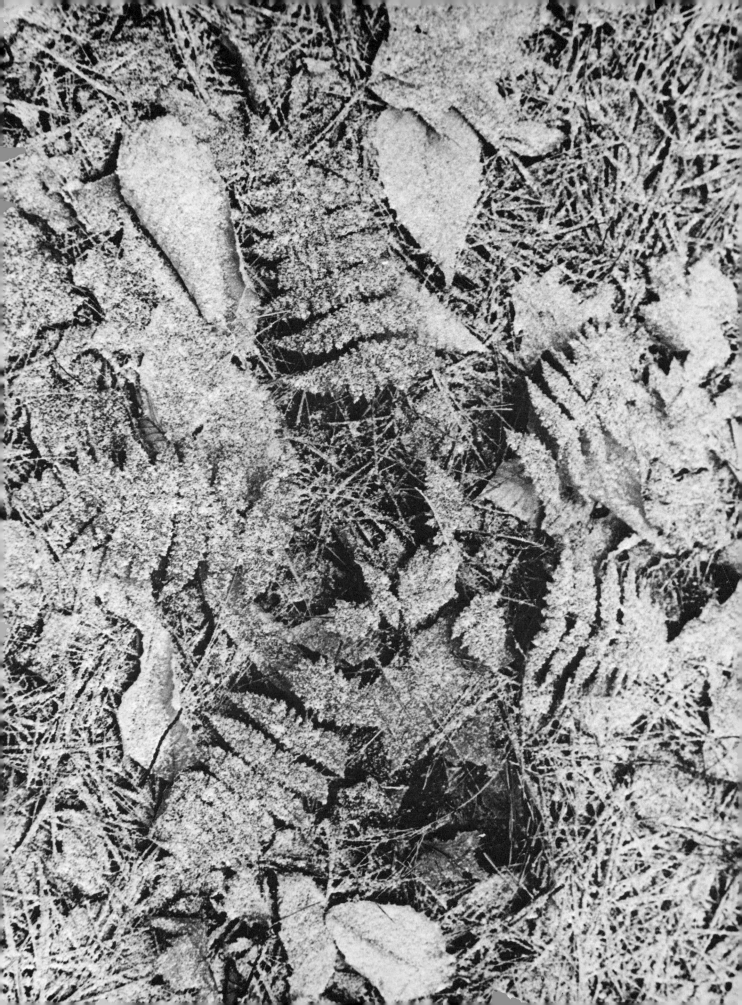

Introduction

HAL BORLAND

THERE MUST HAVE BEEN GOOD reasons for asking me to write an introduction for this book, but neither of the obvious ones is valid. First, because I am not a Vermonter, I presumably would be unbiased. And second, being a naturalist, I probably *would* be biased, since this is a book about nature. But, being a New Englander both by marriage and adoption, I am *biased;* for reasons I shall get to in a moment, I even feel a kind of proprietary interest in Vermont. On the other hand, since a good many naturalists are natural philosophers, the philosopher in me is wary of bias and aims at truth and the long view, especially when it comes to nature. Put it this way: I am pro-nature, but I have my doubts about the belief among some of my friends that Vermont is a mountainous edition of Eden. It has its virtues, but so has my corner of Connecticut.

I first discovered Vermont back in my salad days when I came east from the High Plains and the rugged Rockies. Curious about this fabled New England, the whole of which was only a little more than half the size of my native Colorado, I set out to see it. Driving north past Lake George, I crossed into Vermont, went up to Burlington and Champlain, east to Montpelier, and headed for New Hampshire and Maine.

But roads were less than highways in those days and only the kindness of Vermont farmers saved me from becoming an unwilling Vermonter then and there. They pulled me out of mudholes, fed me, warmed me, smiled at my outland inflection, approved my knowledge of cows and horses, and set me on my way again. I went on across to the Maine coast and back down and around to New York City. I saw New England, at least in part. But I remembered Vermont.

Twenty-odd years later we bought the farm where we still live, here in the northwest corner of Connecticut, and the old Vermont memories came out of hibernation like a woodchuck in April. Vermont's mountains come spilling down across Massachusetts into our dooryard. Her meadowed valleys with snug barns and farmhouses and rocky hillside pastures reach down here, in a sense, with the same wildflowers to sweeten the air and brighten the earth from May until October's splendor overwhelms them, and us. Vermont's sugar maples grow here, to warm our hearts and sweeten our dispositions, and her pines and hemlocks make our lower Berkshires almost as green as Vermont's fabled Green Mountains. Here, too, are white-water brooks and cold blue ponds with trout and pickerel, and in our thickets are deer and bobcats and partridges. Vermont even sent a vast cargo of extra rocks down here when the glaciers were running.

And, to cap it all, we too have Ethan Allen. Ethan was born just down the river from here and for a time, two hundred years or so ago, he ran one of our iron furnaces over in North Canaan. He took quite a company of local boys north with him when Vermont was still the New Hampshire Grants. We still swap yarns about Ethan Allen when we are in the remembering mood. I have made up a few myself.

Do I begin to make it understandable? I hope so, for the things I have to say about this book involve memories and emotions as well as facts. The truth is that I am biased in favor of its underlying philosophy, the implicit statement it makes about conservation, in Vermont, in New England, everywhere.

This book didn't begin as a book, or even as an idea for one. It began back in 1946 as a quarterly magazine called *Vermont Life* and sponsored by the Vermont Development Department. Its purpose was to promote the best interests of the state. How it happened, I don't know, but somehow it succeeded in giving a new and happier meaning to the word "development" by insisting that Vermont's best interests lay in her natural endowments. Instead of boasting about the exploitation of natural resources, it celebrated the way they were being saved and cherished. It devoted itself to conservation, which is another way of saying it has appreciated, in the broadest sense, those aspects of our natural environment which make life worth living despite the urban sprawl and industrial waste and blight.

Over the years, *Vermont Life* has reached a circulation of 125,000 copies, more than enough to put a copy in every home in Vermont. But less than half those copies stay at home; most of them go to readers elsewhere in New England and all over the United States, simply because it is now one of the better magazines about American Wildlife. And now that it has achieved its majority, someone had the good sense to see that there was a worth-while book in its accumulated pages.

This, of course, is that book, and as I read its contents I was satisfied that it is more than a local picture of one corner of New England. That proprietary interest I mentioned was satisfied, for it presents a picture of this whole area's outdoors, its life and natural aspects, its seasons, its mountains and valleys and streams and ponds, its birds and animals and trees and flowers and ferns. And yet, it is also a picture of my own mountainside and valley; and I suspect that, like any good and honest book about such matters, it will ring true, either in fact or memory, for readers elsewhere, even far away.

No book—or magazine, for that matter—is any better than its writers and artists. It is my firm belief that editors need writers the way cooks need pantries. Without the ingredients, the best cook in the world can't make either a stew or a soufflé, no matter how good his recipes. *Vermont Life*'s editors have consistently found able writers and illustrators, some close at home, some in neighboring states, some at a distance. They have been proud of their own but not chauvinistic. The result is excellent.

A good deal of the material here, particularly that dealing with animals, was written by Ronald Rood, a Connecticut native, a graduate biologist, and a Vermonter since 1951. I first met Rood in print in his first book, *Land Alive,* and thought then that here was a man who saw the natural world with keen, fresh eyes and wrote about it with precision and a sense of humor.

He still does, and he sees more and writes better year by year.

Miriam Chapin, another Vermonter, contributed two selections, one a light-hearted piece about porcupines, the other a serious, tantalizing piece about ferns. It tantalizes because even she, who knew her ferns, can only touch the subject's high spots—Vermont, after all, has more than eighty species of ferns, more than any other state in America.

Harold B. Hitchcock writes a piece about caves and their bats. At Middlebury College he is Dr. Hitchcock, chairman of the Biology Department; but in these pages he is a bat-man and a spelunker, articulate and full of unusual information.

George D. Aiken describes typical wildflowers, text to go with the spectacular color photographs of Charles Cleveland Johnson. Mr. Aiken has been United States Senator from Vermont since 1940 and before that he was the state's governor. But he is also a botanist of distinction and once grew wildflowers for a living, even wrote a book about them. How many states can boast of a Senator who knows *Dicentra Cucullaria* from *Dicentra canadensis,* or who can write of skunk cabbage that "it must be of a sensitive nature"?

There are others, quite a few, but I will rest with Edwin Way Teale, Connecticut countryman and Pulitzer prizewinner, who writes about Vermont's sea gulls. Vermont hasn't a foot of seacoast, but it has ring-bill gulls, several thousand of them, and Mr. Teale writes about them with his familiar skill.

Have I given you some idea of this book? What I have tried to say is that it is both Vermont and more than Vermont, for it deals with matters familiar to outdoor people everywhere, even those who must explore vicariously. It deals with the particular, with one small, rugged, mountainous New England state, and yet it deals with the world just beyond all our doorsteps.

What it says, without once raising its voice, is that the natural world around us has satisfactions and assurances for us if we will only accept them and let their freshness and vitality become a part of our lives. Its basic theme is conservation; but conservation, after all, is no more and no less than the attempt to keep this earth habitable and somewhat hospitable for mankind.

The Wild and Curious Bobcat

RONALD ROOD

ROBERT CANDY Illustrations

"MY WIFE AND I SAW IT BESIDE A gravel road near Starksboro. We noticed this big blob of a thing up on a telephone pole. I slowed the car to see what it was. This must have scared it, for it jumped, even though it was nearly twenty feet from the ground. It landed lightly, like a cat, and bounced away like a rabbit."

My neighbor pulled his chin thoughtfully. Then he continued: "It was reddish brown and looked twice the size of a house cat. It's only the second bobcat I've seen in the wild in thirty years."

Actually, a wild, unmolested bobcat every fifteen years is a good average. Many a back-country neighbor of mine has roamed the woods longer than that without ever seeing a 'cat. They're just not that common, although by reputation they lurk around every bend in the trail. Besides, those tufted ears and yellow eyes are sharp enough to warn their owner of your coming long before you arrive. And even if you do surprise a bobcat, its streaked face and spotted body are good camouflage while it peers at you from behind a stump. Then, catlike, it steals away without a sound.

It can be noisy enough when it wants to, however. Bobcats use about the same language as tomcats on a back fence—only several times more so. And when one of them spits and yowls on a distant hillside you're glad there's a valley between you, even if you know there's no clear record of an unprovoked attack on a human.

This vocal prowess in the mating season and the way it lives help make the bobcat so fascinating. It's on a perpetual short fuse. Basking in the sun on a ledge, this twenty-pound cousin of the domestic cat merely looks like an overgrown tabby. Rouse it to anger, though, and it slashes to the attack with canine teeth bared and knifelike claws ready to rip its foe. A Mexican chihuahua probably could put it to flight, but if it's cornered it can whip nearly any dog alive.

Lynx rufus—the scientist's way of saying "the rufous-colored lynx"—is just slightly smaller than its northern cousin, the Canadian lynx, and sometimes may even exceed it in size. It has caterwauled its way at one time or another through most of the United States, the southern edge of Canada and down into Mexico. Here in Vermont it's variously known as wildcat, bay lynx and sometimes as catamount—this last name probably from the French *chat du mont,* "mountain cat," and more often referring to the panther. But, as my friend's roadside experience indicates, it is not confined to the forest. It's found in the swamps, among high ledges, and in overgrown brushland.

Sometimes it's even found near farmyards. In February and March the male goes in search of companionship. Whereas his normal range may take in a square mile, he now may cover twenty-five miles in a single night. His intended mate may not make things any easier, either. She may wander off in the other direction. And since both are gifted with catlike curiosity, they may decide to investigate a nearby farmstead or two in the process.

The wanderings of a bobcat, whether in breeding season or not, are remarkably erratic. Everything tempts its curiosity. It may follow a path for a few feet and then turn to sniff a pebble or a tiny tuft of grass. It may sit in silent absorption, watching the activity of an anthill. Then when its contemplations are finished it may deposit a bit of its own excreta on the anthill as a perverse finishing touch. In good bobcat country, every anthill may be so decorated. At other times, like its small domestic cousin, it carefully covers its wastes with a characteristic "scratch" or "scrape."

When bobcat meets bobcat in the proper season, the results are likely to be deafening. Shouting sweet nothings at each other, they plight their troth at the top of their lungs. Once they've paired, however, they may travel together quietly, sneaking up on a rabbit or ground-nesting bird in complete silence.

A hunting bobcat is a study in concentration. It may try several different approaches to its prey, perhaps to determine which is best. As it crouches, its abbreviated six-inch tail twitches in anticipation. Finally, with a rush, it pounces.

If the prey eludes that first dash, it may escape completely. The bobcat relies on surprise rather than speed. Losing the first rabbit, it philosophically goes about finding another. Sometimes a trail in the snow shows several such near-misses. If it catches more than enough for a meal—such as a wounded deer—it often covers up the remainder and returns for more later.

About two months after mating and hunting, the female puts an end to the

2

From left: Black bear sleeping in the open against a ledge; sparrow hawks (kestrels) are good little hawks, which return early; a shrew, which forages all winter.

tightly woven moth cocoon. A gray "berry" in a bush was the silken chamber of a resting spider. A slab of bark that came off in my hand as I pulled myself over a ledge uncovered a whole insect zoo—drowsy flies, slow-moving beetles, yellow bark-borers, even a tightly folded moth.

Something unusual about an abandoned bird's nest caught my eye. It looked big and bulky, almost as if it had been used two seasons, something birds seldom do. It was roofed over with leaves and grass.

I pulled it closer to examine it. There was an outraged squeak from inside. Then out popped a furry head with two large dark eyes. I released the bush hastily. One of Vermont's most widespread creatures was at home, but not to visitors—the white-footed deer mouse, ranging in winter from a pile of newspapers in the attic to this re-modeled bird's nest in the woods.

Other sleeping creatures were around us, too—in the hollows of trees, hidden in ledges, or safe underground. I recall a chipmunk I saw some years ago. It had curled up in its underground burrow for the winter, when, shortly after Thanksgiving, a bulldozer had unearthed it. It was so profoundly asleep that it could be tossed back and forth like a baseball.

Somewhere in other burrows were skunks and woodchucks. Bears snoozed in their hollow trees. Bats hung like dried fruit from the sides of caves in a dozen parts of the state.

We came upon a porcupine den in a ledge. The snow was all melted around the entrance where it led down between two rocks. The single-file tracks of a fox mingled with those of the quill-pigs as they sauntered forth to a tasty tree. It had nosed the den, but had wisely continued on its way.

Following the fox trail, we found where it had investigated the cubbyhole—called a "form"—of a snowshoe hare under a spruce. Then it sniffed beneath a pine where a red squirrel had sat in the branches, shelling the cones. From there its tracks took us to the edge of the woods where, doglike, it trotted from one stump to another. We saw where it had pounced on a clump of grass in hopes of finding a mouse nest. Then its tracks turned back into the woods.

Tom tossed a snowball at a haystack. At once a dozen sparrows flew out. They had learned to make good use of this pile of food and warmth. And near by were two ponies, with yesterday's snow still on their backs. Their coats had grown so thick that the body heat had not gone through. They, too, were dressed for winter.

7

The Indians called this the "hungry time." It was brought by a wicked witch, Squaw Winter. She pinched the stomachs of foxes and wolves, making them chew on bark and sticks to ease the cramp. Sometimes she sent the great white owls down from the arctic when food was scarce in the north—something she still does occasionally in Vermont. She made the deer "yard up" in sheltered areas, trampling the snow down in their self-made enclosure and hesitating to leave even if condemning themselves to starvation.

Preparation for the hungry time sometimes takes place far in advance. One spring a killing frost blanketed the countryside. The delicate green of the trees turned to an ugly gray. But in scarcely a week the green was back. The first thing many a plant does as it opens its buds is to start preparing for a complete new set of buds as an emergency measure. Usually they are not called for until the following spring, but they are ready —insulating scales and all—even before the current crop of leaves has taken full form.

One fall day we watched a grasshopper prepare in her own way for the winter ahead. She thrust her abdomen deep into the ground, remaining thus for several minutes. Later we carefully dug up the spot and found her eggs. They were packed side by side like tiny well-placed grains of rice. Soon the frost would blot out her life and that of millions of her species, and not a single one of her kind would be left in the state of Vermont. Then their entire future on this planet would depend on those silent, unmoving eggs.

So it is each winter with numbers of our insects who fling the torch of life to a generation yet unborn—gypsy moths, tent caterpillars, praying mantises, and many species of aphids and beetles.

Squaw Winter cannot touch the snail beneath the rock with the entrance to its shell glazed over, nor the mole and its earthworm prey below the frostline. And winter means little to the young queen hornet who, alone of all her thousands of brothers and sisters, remains to start a new paper nest. Hiding under a bit of bark, she sometimes takes a piece of wood between her jaws, like a child taking a toy to bed.

Then there was the time we thought we saw a woodchuck which had come out in January.

It was a warm day. The river was swollen with melted snow. I pointed my binoculars toward our hillside. Sure enough, poking along over a patch of bare ground, was a woodchuck—Old Groundhog himself. Looking into its habits later, I discovered some startling things about this process called hibernation.

True hibernation brings about an awesome change in an animal. The heart may beat only three or four times a minute, breathing may be impossible to detect, and the blood courses so slowly that a cut will not bleed. The body processes may slow down to one one-hundredth of their normal speed. Bats, chipmunks and woodchucks may hibernate, but few of the other animals do—and that includes the "hibernating" black bear, which is only drowsing.

Even hibernating animals are sensitive to touch, strange as this may seem. Perhaps the fact explains our unusual visitor in the meadow. Some perennially active mole may have blundered into the 'chuck's burrow below the frostline and poked around enough to waken it.

Some of the winter creatures never slow completely to a stop. Any warm day brings out "snow fleas," little dark insects whose smoky-colored bodies absorb the sun's heat. Sometimes a garter snake can be seen sunning itself on a stone wall. Even the spring peeper, tiny cousin of the frogs in the mud, and the toads buried underground, may

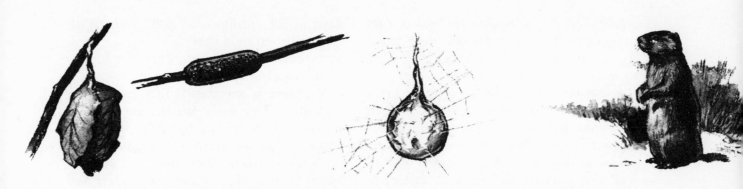

From left: Polyphemus moth cocoon, tent caterpillar eggs, egg sac of the garden spider, and Old Groundhog himself.

call from the woods during a thaw.

But the worst case of insomnia is that of the wood turtle. It is a confirmed wanderer. In the summer we often see it walking along the edge of a country road—ground-colored shell, yellow and black underneath. One winter day the ice was free of snow on a brook near our house. We put on our skates and bumped along over the rippled ice. Suddenly the children got down on their knees and peered through the ice. There, on the bottom, was a wood turtle, still wandering.

There can be nothing much colder than a cold-blooded reptile plodding through ice water. Yet there it is, most of the winter, slowly making its way over the bottom. What it's looking for, nobody knows.

Perhaps seven out of ten birds we saw in summer have gone south for the winter. The bobolink of our hayfields is in northern Argentina. The barn swallow may be in Brazil. But many of the birds appear to be on a more limited travel budget, going only to the Carolinas or, at most, Florida. Some do not go even that far. Connecticut bird-lovers, for instance, feed our Vermont juncos all winter.

There's another kind of migration. My home in the mountains is some fifteen miles from the Champlain Valley, as the crow flies. And the crow flies it, too, every

fall—a vertical migration of only a few hundred feet in altitude, but nonetheless a migration. We can expect no crows in Lincoln until late February.

Each spring we catch a few trout in our pasture stream. Yet by July the stream is just a dry gravel bed. But with fall and winter it begins to flow; and the trout enter it from where it joins the river, following the ancestral urge to work upstream. While the brooks are locked under a blanket of snow, natural restocking is going on all over Vermont.

There's still another migration. We saw its beginnings one day as we were crossing Lake Champlain on a ferry. A straggling of orange-and-black butterflies winged over the lake, scorning the rest offered by the superstructure of the boat. They were the Monarch butterflies, whose life began as caterpillars on our Vermont milkweeds, and would continue during the winter along the Atlantic Coast. Weighing but a fraction of an ounce, they yet have the power to fly across large bodies of water—unique insect migrants, making a round trip of hundreds of miles.

Their adaptation to winter is no more strange, perhaps, than that of our valuable insect, the honeybee. It supplies its own warmth. Forming a ball of individuals in the hive, the bees keep warm by increased

9

activity. As the inner ones are heated, they move outward, and others take their place. Their movement requires honey for energy, so the beekeeper leaves them enough.

Sometimes interloper mice try to make their way into the warmth of the hive. If they are caught in time, they are promptly stung to death. But the bees now have a corpse to dispose of. So they cover it with wax and propolis, or bee glue, fashioned from the resin of buds. In the spring the beekeeper opens the hive and finds the intruder, sealed in an airtight mummy-case.

One night there was a knock at my door. "I found something in my wastebasket," said my neighbor from down the road. "What is it, and where did it come from?"

We carefully tipped the basket out in a dry sink. Smaller than a mouse, running in what seemed to be all directions, was the creature most directly the opposite of the drowsy winter animals. It was a shrew. Like all shrews, it was desperately hungry. I tossed in a piece of hamburger; it gobbled it up almost without pausing. Hunger had driven it in from the fields. Hunger drives the weasel from the tough going of the deep snow to the wealth of the chicken-house, and causes the mice to girdle the fruit trees at ground level—something they seldom do in summer. Hunger, too, sometimes leads the fox along the highway in broad daylight in search of some crumb from a passing car.

Several winters ago the water in our cistern became cloudy. Uncovering the spring which supplied it, we found the evidence of a frantic chase. A mink, ranging far from its usual haunts in the river several hundred feet away, had captured the trout we kept in the spring to keep it clean. With the ice frozen solid over the river, the mink sometimes has to look elsewhere for food—in this case our spring.

Yet there is one animal that may get fat in winter. This is the beaver, our familiar aquatic engineer. His fur is so thick and resistant that he can swim through ice water with no apparent discomfort. All the autumn he has labored, cutting poplars and willows for food, stuffing their green branches butt first in the mud. Then, when the pond is frozen solid, he merely swims out under the ice to his food cache and helps himself. Deep within the lodge that seems to be but a mound of snow at the edge of the water, he feasts until spring.

We have found out much about our winter creatures. But the prediction as to what kind of a winter we are likely to be having is still anybody's guess. The thickness of the scales on winter buds is supposed to tell, as is the layer of fat on the saddle of a bear, the thickness of the hair on a cow. But the most reliable indicator of all, according to the old-timers, is the famous woolly bear caterpillar.

Wearing a bristly crew cut that is brown in the center and black at both ends, the woolly bear is eagerly watched for a forecast of the winter to come. The wider the center band, say some weather prophets, the more open and snowless the winter will be. Others disagree: the bigger the band the bigger the snowdrifts.

How does the woolly bear feel about its own predictions? Unaffected by the controversy, it finds a pile of leaves in a hollow tree. Then quietly retiring from sight, it curls up until spring.

Winter

SONJA BULLATY and ANGELO LOMEO:

An Essay in Black and White

Clockwise, starting at the top left, are: Long-eared owl, Great Horned owl, Saw-whet owl, Barred owl, Screech owl and arctic Snowy owl.

Wings That Swoop in the Night

RONALD ROOD: *On Owls*

ROBERT CANDY Illustrations

THE SCREAMS OF SOME OF THEM have chilled campers around a fire. The musical trills of others have sealed lovers' pledges under a summer moon. Their fantastic hearing has enabled them to snatch mice from tunnels in the snow. And their silent presence in roadside trees has caused auto crashes when drivers craned their necks for a better look. In short, no matter where an owl may be or what it does, it is likely to have a profound effect on the world around it.

Take those screams, for instance. You're lucky if you get to hear them once or twice in a lifetime—maybe luckier if you don't. If you happen to camp near a nest where young barred owls or great horned owls have just started to fly, you may be serenaded most of the night. Or you may merely be out for a woodland walk on a gray afternoon when one of them lets forth its unearthly shriek—filling you with thoughts of bobcats, panthers, and escaped maniacs.

Actually, owls can be surprisingly vocal. But you've got to be where you can hear them at the right time. They're at their best from dusk to dawn, when most people are inside the house. They have an impressive repertory, and a number of their noises just don't sound as if they could come from an owl.

The saw-whet owl sounds like a file be-

ing used with short, decisive strokes; in the distance it sounds almost like a little bell. Barn owls hiss like radiators, while long-eared owls can coo like doves and short-eared owls may squeal like pigs. And the little screech owl has anything but a screech. Its quavery, down-sliding whistle has been called one of the pleasantest night sounds in all of nature.

The two owls that sound more or less as an owl should are the great horned and the barred varieties. The great horned owl's regular call is three or five unaccented hoots—often so low in pitch that they sound like the grunts of a large animal. The barred owl, or "eight-hooter," as it's sometimes called, has a measured cadence of four hoots, a pause, and four more, ending in a descending sound almost like a crow's caw. Ask in a slow, moderately high voice: "Who cooks for you? Who cooks for you-all?" and you've got the sound made by this, our most common large owl. Distance can play tricks on hearing, though, since from far off the barred owl sounds like a barking dog.

But owls aren't merely good noisemakers. In fact, they're usually silent as they go about their business. Silence helps them to swoop down on mice, frogs and other creatures—often in pitch darkness and guided by little more than the rustle of leaves below them.

17

We once had a barn owl that had injured a wing. For the month or so that we nursed it back to health, we learned much about these birds. Titus, as we called him from his scientific name, *Tyto alba,* had the typically huge, staring eyes and fixed expression. His face was oddly flattened, with the heart-shaped facial disc which gives the barn owl its alias of "monkey-faced owl."

Like most owls he was soft and fluffy—with the exception, of course, of his taloned feet. Each foot had two toes forward and two to the rear. As an added efficiency, one rear toe on each foot could swivel in either direction as needed for a better grip.

Our interest in Titus led us to read all we could find on owls. We discovered that everything about an owl fits it precisely for its specialized way of life. Nothing is wasted. It is as functional as an eggbeater—or a steel trap.

Camera fans know that a huge lens usually means a superb camera. The eyes of owls, like great lenses, capture the slightest flicker of light in the gloom. The two-foot-tall snowy owl, a rare visitor from the Arctic Circle, has eyes almost as big as a human's.

As we watched Titus, we discovered that he had to turn his head to look from side to side. His eyes, in owl fashion, were fixed in their sockets. But we found this is probably not the disadvantage that it seems. This is where the concave facial disc, typical of all owls, comes in. Near the edge of the disc is the hidden ear opening. Whenever you have cupped your ear to hear a sound better, your hand was performing what is the likely function of each disc. Scientists think it serves as a perpetual sound scoop, channeling every whisper of noise back to the ear.

And as the owl turns its head to hear the sound better, the eyes are always boring in the same direction, helping the ears.

Some owls even have one ear opening larger than the other, so the sound is pinpointed further with every slight shift of their heads.

Their hearing is amazing. Put a barn owl in a pitch-black room with the carcass of a mouse tied to a string. Nothing happens. Then pull the string slightly, so the mouse rustles a few bits of paper on the floor and *wham!*— the owl has landed on it.

When you see an owl take wing, you're struck by its silent mothlike flight. Here, again, everything fits. It used to be thought that the "mufflers," or soft fringes, on an owl's feathers were to prevent its prey from hearing it approach. But the purpose may be more than that: the mufflers may help the owl to "tiptoe" through the air, and listen without being distracted by the whispering of the wind in its feathers.

The tiniest owl of our region is the saw-whet—a robin-sized creature so tame that you can pick it up in your hand. The largest you are likely to see is the great horned owl, two feet tall and so savage that it will battle anything in the sky but an airplane. In between are the others already mentioned, plus the occasional snowy owl down from the north when its supply of lemmings and arctic hares becomes scarce.

Owls are great opportunists as far as food is concerned. Almost anything that moves is fair prey. Most other birds settle down at night while mice and small animals are active; the owls' nocturnal activity helps account for their banner record as the world's best mousetraps.

Much of the harsh opinion about owls is due to the fiercest of them all—the great horned owl. This soldier of fortune disclaims the usual owl diet, heavy in rodents. It has a more cosmopolitan taste, as you might suspect from its free-swinging habits. It sees perfectly well by day (as do most owls, really), although it prefers subdued

18

light, and it may soar over a meadow like a hawk. Thus a whole new menu is spread below—rabbits, game birds, snakes, poultry. It has even been known to dive for fish like an osprey.

Life starts early in the year for this great owl, as with most of its kin. Courtship may take place in late January or early February. It's a tender affair. After preening his lady's feathers with his bill, carrying on with piercing screams, and flying around her in aerial gymnastics, the male may find his efforts rewarded when she preens and screams back. They may seal the pact with a feast on a passing rabbit. Soon they nest.

For many owls, almost anything will do for a nest. Great horned owls will nest in a hollow tree, perhaps, or under an overhanging ledge. They will also take last year's crow's nest. Even the massive nests of bald eagles, high in a tree and used year after year by the rightful owners, may be usurped by the great horned owl. If the eagles protest, the owl spreads its wings, snaps its beak viciously in typical owl fashion and refuses to vacate.

The couple pins its hopes on two or three round, whitish eggs laid in February or March. One time I found a female owl incubating in the top of a broken stump.

The snow was drifting, and I would never have seen her if she hadn't turned her head.

The female sits on the eggs through snow and cold. Her mate gives the marriage vows at least beak-service and brings food for them both to share. Occasionally he may spell her for a few hours on the eggs, but mostly he just lingers near by.

The young hatch in about a month if the eggs don't freeze. Like most baby owls, they're all beaks and claws and are covered with a thick suit of downy underwear. And, like any baby birds, they're gifted with bottomless appetites.

Now the parents fly practically a shuttle service from food source to nest. If a poultry yard happens to be near at hand, the toll of half-grown and even adult chickens may be great. Nor is it always chickens. Underneath one horned owl's tree were the bodies of one hundred thirteen barn rats. The heads had been eaten, the rest cast away.

Other kinds of food found in and about this owl's nests include weasels, small woodchucks, and birds. He's even been known to pick up a stray cat here and there. And there's one item the owl seems fond of despite an obvious drawback—the skunk. Apparently a skunk snatched from above

19

has little chance to use its weapon, and owls have a poor sense of smell, anyway. So a skunk makes a perfect dinner target in the dusk—white stripes and all.

Of course after a few skunk dinners the nest reeks of the odor—especially during a rain. My father had a stuffed horned owl in our attic when I was small; when the rain leaked in on it one time the smell was so powerful that Mother made him put it out in the barn.

Owls often bolt their food whole. This practice could lead to awkward gastronomic problems of what to do with bones, claws, hair and feathers. But the owls have their own neat solution: the indigestible parts are merely rolled into a little ball in the stomach and cast back up again in the form of pellets. When I was a forestry student, we analyzed the contents of a number of these pellets—not only to determine what owls ate, but also to learn the relative abundance of different species of mice and small mammals of the forest. Our analyses disclosed the presence of a certain pine mouse that was unknown in that part of Connecticut until its remains were discovered in some owl pellets.

The heap of pellets accumulates around the owl's nest as the weeks go by. The young owls grow in size, but are slow to produce feathers—which helps explain why most owls have to get such an early start in the spring. Even though a young owl is flightless, it can defend itself. Sitting on its haunches or even rolling over on its back, an owl of any size presents little else but a snapping beak and hooked claws that can strike out with lightning speed.

Until the time of flight things are fairly quiet in most owl families. The adults are usually silent in the vicinity of the nest. Their earlier spring concerts have lapsed into occasional calls to each other in the darkened forest. But when the young leave home the vocalizing picks up again. Barred and horned owls may follow the parents around, shrieking and hooting enough to warn all prey for acres. Other owls do little better with their assortment of noises.

One night we heard a commotion in our old cherry tree, and when we went outside, there sat five screech owls in a row on a limb, practicing the shivery, descending scales typical of the species. As they turned their heads, the sound seemed to float all over the tree. If each one had been sitting in a fork right next to the trunk, which is common owl practice, we might not have found them at all. The sound was confusing even while we looked right at them.

Owls usually stay hidden during the day, but sometimes sharp eyes spy them out. One afternoon we saw a great flock of crows, flapping and cawing and diving at the top of an old dead tree stub. As we watched, trying to figure out the cause of the ruckus, the end of the stub suddenly detached itself and flew off into the forest. It had been an owl, probably sunning itself with lids lowered over its great eyes, until the crows put an end to its nap.

Indeed, so bitter is the feud between crows and owls that crow-hunters often put a papier-mâché owl in a convenient spot and then wait for the crows to discover it. I have seen screech owls mobbed the same way, too. Interestingly, the attacks were made by comparatively small birds: jays, starlings, sparrows. Thus the little owl, no larger than a pigeon with a shortened tail, had attracted a host of tormentors commensurate with its own size.

But when dusk comes, the attackers fade away. They retire to their perches and leave the world to the owls. From then until sunup, these birds of prey range the darkened countryside almost unseen, unheard, and unknown—which, for a feathered mousetrap, is just the way it should be.

The Fish That Shouldn't Be There

RONALD ROOD: *On Smelt*

YOU'VE GOT TO HAND IT TO THE smelt. With more odds stacked up against it than a fish ought to have, it's surprising that it hasn't dropped out of the Vermont scene long ago. Yet it not only holds its own, but even runs to astonishing numbers in favored spots.

This is all the more interesting when you realize that the smelt probably doesn't belong here in the first place. Look in a

used smelt as bait for lake trout for nothing. While many small fish stay in the safety of the shallows, the smelt spends much of its time in the cool deeps. Therefore it is handy to the appetite of its huge cousin. And its young are potential fare for almost everything that swims.

Perhaps the biggest hazard occurs in the early spring. "Smelt really have a big job to do at spawning time," a fisheries man

book of natural history and you'll find it listed as "a salt-water fish, about six to fourteen inches long, ascending rivers and estuaries to spawn." Our Lake Champlain smelt probably were landlocked in the postglacial period, after the lake lost its direct sea connection to the north. Hence they occur in Champlain naturally.

How smelt made it into most other Green Mountain lakes is another question, although a few have been stocked in the past by the Fish and Game Department. They are there, in any event, in Memphremagog, Bomoseen and a dozen other Vermont waters.

Getting here, however, turned out to be just the start of things. Fishermen hadn't

told me. "Those that have made it through the winter have to head for the streams which enter the lake. They gather at the mouth in great numbers. I've seen them so thick that you couldn't tell how far below them the bottom was.

"Then they go upriver to spawn on gravel and underwater objects. The males often go first and mill around, waiting for the females. Lucky for them they congregate at night when most of their enemies can't see them. Otherwise the slaughter would be terrific."

When the masses of smelt have worked upstream, spawning takes place. Pressure of the ripened eggs within the female's body is sometimes aided by pressure of the bodies of one or more attendant males. Pinhead size, the eggs are scattered over the gravel, on stones, on underwater objects.

With millions of eggs lying around like so much sticky underwater sand, the egg-eaters have a feast. Crustaceans, aquatic insects and a host of different kinds of fish find wonderful picking. Day by day the harvest continues even as the tiny young are developing within the egg.

It is fortunate for the species that a two-ounce smelt can produce up to five thousand eggs, because everything seems to like smelt caviar. Fishermen have netted minnows crammed to the throat with smelt eggs.

In about ten days—more or less, according to weather and water conditions—the fry emerge. Their enemies follow them as they drift downstream to the comparative safety of lake water.

During this period nature relents a little. She gives them a food sac of a tiny yolk mass from the egg. This sac remains attached for a few days until absorbed; then they must find the plankton and other minute creatures they use as food. Also, their transparency gives them a protective cloak of near invisibility.

Hatched in water which was about 40 degrees Fahrenheit when the eggs were laid, the fry now follow the cool stream-flow out into the lake. Here, instead of minnows and diving beetles as enemies, they have pike, lake trout and perch.

At this point the wheel of nature begins to turn in their favor. As they turn adolescent, they adopt the sleek, silvery, streamlined bodies which show their distant kinship to the salmon. Their mouths develop sharp, back-slanting teeth, enabling them to hang onto an assortment of crustaceans, underwater insects and plankton.

Then, when they're finally large enough, the wheel comes full circle. With almost an avenging gleam in its eye, the now sizable smelt may turn and snap up the young of its old enemy, the lake trout.

This could all be a case of a simple balance of nature, with one creature serving as a necessary check on the other, if several thousand human beings didn't enter the picture. A city springs up almost overnight when the Champlain ice gets thick enough to hold the fishing shanties. I'm told that smelt make more "fishing widows" per pound than all the other species combined.

Now the smelt find a new hazard. This is in the form of a hook rigged with a chunk of pork or a slab cut from another smelt's side, jigging up and down at the end of some sixty-five or more feet of line. The smelt, cruising around in great numbers, watch the antics of this strange piece of material for a while.

Finally, with luck—good or bad, depending on whose viewpoint you use—the little fish takes hold. Swiftly it is hauled up to the surface, perhaps to reappear in a short time as a fresh slab of bait. Sometimes the fisherman pulls it up so quickly that even if the hook hasn't caught, the smelt hasn't time to extricate its teeth from the bait.

Although the school is often far below the surface, it may sometimes come right to the top, possibly because of an oxygen deficiency. Then its huge numbers become startlingly evident. "I recall my father telling me about a hole he dug in the ice near Ferrisburg," a friend told me. "He was chopping it to get a bucket of water. Just as he punched the last hole through, he noticed that the water was alive with some little fish. In his curiosity, he scooped at them and caught a couple. They were smelt —apparently swimming around by the thousands. So he and a friend scooped away as fast as they could with a pail until there were dozens of smelt lying all around them on the ice."

Pails, and many other assorted items, are now regarded as illegal by the Fish and Game Department. Smelt are usually taken by angling in Vermont although dip nets are permitted in a few places. Not so in some other states of our Northeast which share this marine heritage, however. There, throngs of silent fishermen line the darkened banks of rivers in early spring, quietly waiting a signal. Then, lights flash on and the water foams as fishermen (and fisher-

"silversides," the smelt bears the scientific name of *Osmerus mordax*. But it is most familiarly known from an old Anglo-Saxon term, "smoelt," which means "beautiful." This is an apt term for the slightly transparent, silver-green being that lances through the waters of our eastern coasts from Virginia north to Nova Scotia and inland to the Great Lakes. In these latter bodies of water, it spawns on wave-washed shores, especially in Ontario and Erie.

women) swish through the water with nets, dip nets or "scaps," frames of chicken wire, even bedsprings. The light-shy smelt, caught on the way to their breeding sites, are packed so thick that they cannot escape. But in spite of this blow at their numbers, enough pairs escape to leave a few million fertile eggs behind. And so their populations continue, apparently none the worse for the weeding-out process.

Taking the smelt during their river run is no new idea. It's a time-honored custom here on the east coast, as well as in the west coast and European waters. According to an account by Captain John Smith, "Of smelts there is such abundance that the Salvages doe take them up in the rivers with baskets, like sives."

What causes this apparent mania for a fish which is only about twice the size of your thumb? "I don't know," shrugged one fisherman. "It's just a wonderful way to spend a winter's day, I guess. But did you ever taste a good fresh smelt? It's awful hard to beat. Nothing tastes quite like it. It's sweet, somehow, and not fishy like other fish. In fact, it has a pleasant odor, almost like cucumbers, when it's first caught."

Variously called locally "frostfish" and

One big mystery of the Champlain smelt, though, is just where they spawn. Even the Fish and Game Department has never found spawning runs in the rivers; yet they find smelt loaded with eggs in water only forty feet deep. The supposition is that these fish spawn at a considerable depth.

Meantime, in spite of the mystery, fishermen continue to harvest the tasty delicacies. "Take a good 'green' smelt, right out of the water," my informative fisherman told me, "dip it in egg and breadcrumbs, and fry it 'til it's brown. Nothing better. Doesn't taste a bit like those frozen, fishy-eyed, gutted things you buy in the market."

"You mean to tell me you dip the fish in the batter whole? Just as nature made it —innards and all?" I asked.

He looked at me as if I'd asked him whom he voted for in the last election. "Of course," he said without batting an eye. "Don't have to add a thing. They're good enough as it is."

I have my own ideas about uncensored smelt. But on one thing I will agree with him. No matter where they spawn or how they're taken, they're uncommonly well named—in the old Anglo-Saxon, that is. For they *are* beautiful—swimming or sizzling.

The Making of Lake Champlain

WALTER R. HARD, JR.

CLEMENS KALISCHER Photographs

BACK IN THE DIM RECESSES OF time, a half-billion years ago, what is now the Champlain area perhaps more resembled the moon. The ancient, pre-Cambrian mountains, the Adirondacks, were there, but towered much higher than now. Nothing was living on the land.

There occurred at this time a profound geologic movement just east of the mountains. The earth's crust slowly buckled and bent downward, forming a deep, north-south trough which actually persists today.

The sea invaded the slowly sinking area and, in the course of millions of years, deposited thousands of feet of sand, clay and mud into this ocean-linked trough. These sediments, after many thousands of years more, finally turned into rock. An example of this new rock is the red sandstone now seen bared at Burlington.

Perhaps 440 million years ago this Champlain area lifted again above the water. Eighty million more years passed and, as the region subsided once more, the marine waters overspread.

The earth's crust again began to feel a deep disturbance. The rocks which had formed in the Champlain trough now were thrust up to form the Taconic mountains. Relentless compressing and folding forced whole beds of ancient rock upward and atop the younger. Such is the Rock Point Overthrust just north of Burlington, one of the outstanding geological phenomena in America. (A painting of it hangs in Bur-

lington's Fleming Museum.) Later, to the east of the Champlain area, deep-lying, molten granite forced itself upward. These intrusions formed the great granite de-

---

The Lake's Vital Statistics

LENGTH: 118 miles, from Whitehall, N.Y., to top of Missisquoi Bay in Quebec.

WIDTH: ½ mile to 10 miles, maximum.

AREA: 490 square miles—322 in Vermont, 151 in New York, 17 in Quebec —including 80 islands totaling 55 square miles.

SHORELINE: 238 miles in Vermont, 170 in New York, about 14 in Quebec.

ELEVATION: water surface averages 95 feet above sea level.

DISCHARGE: 2,992 gallons per second, into Richelieu River on the Canadian side of the border (thus "down" lake is north, "up" is south).

DRAINAGE AREA: 8,277 square miles.

DEPTH: maximum 399 feet, 2 miles north of Split Rock (opposite Charlotte).

FREEZES: average date of freeze-over is February 7; last area to freeze is 3 miles south of Juniper Island (outside Burlington harbor). Lake has failed to freeze over about 15 winters in the last 150.

Cambrian rock overthrust atop younger shale, on Grand Isle.

posits at Barre and the monadnocks such as Mt. Ascutney, even farther east.

At the close of this time, perhaps 200 million years ago, the thrusting and folding of the rocks pushed up into the Green Mountain range—much higher then than now. For uncounted millennia mountains have successively been built up and worn down in this region. The most recent edition of the Green Mountains thus was made largely from the eroded rubble of earlier great ranges.

In comparatively recent days—150 million years ago—the Champlain area came into an era of very mild weather. Lush vegetation covered the land and sustained the Vermont dinosaurs. Notable are the deposits of lignite (a primitive coal) and ochers laid down at the close of this time in the Brandon area.

Recent happenings began perhaps 1 million B.C. as the Great Ice Cap covered all of Vermont. The crushing ice, thousands of feet thick, depressed the land six hundred feet or more by sheer weight. Finally the earth grew warmer and the mountain tops emerged from the ice.

As it lies today Champlain is an infant by geologic reckoning, perhaps less than twelve thousand years old. While the great ice sheet slowly melted, down and northward, it lay for centuries in the Champlain trough. Thus a lake of melted ice was formed in the valley immediately south of the receding glacier.

The lake basin filled. For thousands of years the water, contained at the north end by the ice barrier, drained southward into what is now the Hudson Valley. The south end of the lake, as one still can trace, was held by a natural dam near what is now Schuylerville, New York.

In this stage of time the lake, which has been termed "Lake Vermont," was much higher than now. Many evidences of it re-main to this day—marooned deltas, wave caves, and shoreline terraces such as those clearly defined on the slopes of Mt. Philo, near Charlotte. Eastward, Lake Vermont reached Richmond, Hinesburg and Huntington. An arm extended to Brandon and engulfed Lake Dunmore, near Middlebury. The land level still was partly depressed and even the hilltop campus of the University of Vermont would have been under two hundred feet of water.

As the glacier melted back north of Burlington a new, lower outlet for the lake broke out at Fort Ann, near Whitehall. The lake level dropped. Now the shoreline was at Middlebury's college campus, at Williston and St. Albans. Wave terraces of this lower lake can be seen also on Mt. Philo and other slopes. This second lake remained for more thousands of years.

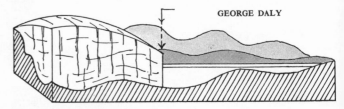

GEORGE DALY

Glacier receding northward (left) held lake (at arrow) to high level. It drained southward to Hudson River. Green Mountains are behind.

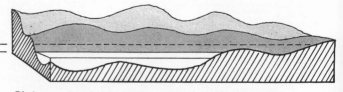

Glacier now is melted back and water floods in from the north.

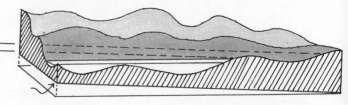

Tilt of the land (dotted lines) cut off the sea. This lake of today barely drains northward. Continued tilt will cause south flow again.

Brick-colored remnant of ancient Sandrock Hills, south of Burlington.

Finally the ice melted back to the valley of the St. Lawrence River—at that time an ocean estuary, depressed by the weight of nearby ice. Then the salt sea flooded south, in front of the old glacier, into the Champlain Valley. With it came the ocean denizens, some of which still survive here: the ling, sheepshead, bowfin and lamprey.

Slowly the ice-relieved land continued to lift as the glacier wasted farther away northward. North of Rouses Point a rocky area made the sea bottom shallow. This area, still rising, finally blocked off the sea's arm from the north. The south end of the lake, meanwhile, had risen still more. So the now fresh-water lake, fed by mountain streams, found its outlet spilling over this northern barrier to flow by the Richelieu River into the St. Lawrence. This is Lake Champlain today.

But slow, relentless forces of nature still move. If this upward spring of the earth continues in the north, geologists say, the balance some day will shift again.

Already the mouths of Otter and Dead creeks, southward on the lake, are flooded back. A geologically minded skin diver off Port Henry will find a not-so-ancient river delta under sixty feet of water.

A further tilt along Champlain's length of only four-tenths of an inch per mile would do it. That would be enough to cause Champlain once again to pour its water southward into the Hudson. But it isn't a matter of immediate concern: A.D. 14,000 would be a likely date.

The Champlain country has milder weather than its neighbors both east and west. It has a longer growing season (one hundred fifty days), less snowfall (four to eight feet) and less rainfall (thirty-four inches). Though the ancient weakness of the earth, which caused Champlain's trough and the building of its neighbor mountains, remains, the scar seems healed.

It is likely that Champlain's clear waters for ages more will continue to temper the valley's climate and pour out its bounties.

27

Fisher-Cat

RONALD ROOD: *On the Porcupine's Nemesis*

ROBERT CANDY Illustration

"WHEN I NUDGED THAT PORCU-pine with my foot I got a big surprise," a logger was telling me. "He'd been sliced down the middle almost as if with a knife. Then he was hollowed out from the underside the way you'd scoop out a muskmelon.

"It wasn't really a porcupine at all—just an empty skin."

I recognized the description at once. This could be the work of only one living creature. Some call it the "black cat" because of its feline appearance and grace. Others call it the "fisher-cat," or simply the "fisher." But no matter by what name it is called locally, *Martes pennanti* is the best porcupine trap ever known in the North Woods.

It will scamper up a sugar maple and slash at a treed porcupine from the underside. A hunter in Essex County once saw this happen. He was sitting on a streamside log, waiting to see what would come past. He looked up and saw a porcupine in a tree fork.

"Then a fisher went up after it, like a big black squirrel," he recalled. "The porcupine bristled and slapped with its tail, but it never touched the fisher. I never saw an animal so quick.

"All of a sudden there was a fight up there. The fisher-cat ran back down the tree like a streak. It had hardly touched ground before the porcupine came crashing down. From the way it fell, I think it was dead before it landed.

"I sneaked over to have a look. But the fisher must have heard me. By the time I got there, a dead porcupine was the only thing there. He was opened up from his throat to his tail."

Although the fisher is the sworn enemy of the porky (food studies show that one fisher stomach in three contains a meal of porcupine), it is able to take nearly anything it fancies as food. It can catch a snowshoe hare; it's so nimble that it often feeds on the red squirrel. It has been called the fastest treetop mammal in North America.

Yet the only fisher-cat of my experience was poking along a lake shore. In spite of its common name, it doesn't catch living fish, but looks for dried ones in the débris. At other times it feeds on berries and fruits. A born economist, it carefully hides any extra food for next time.

My lakeshore specimen was typical in its appearance. Brown-black, with luxuriant fur and a bushy, tapering tail, it was about three feet in over-all length. Its small rounded ears were almost hidden in the

fur. Mine was probably a male, as it was somewhat grizzly gray about the head. Fully adult, it must have weighed nine or ten pounds. Females are evenly colored and smaller, weighing five or six pounds.

A district forester told me of his meeting with a fisher. "I'll never forget the sight of him," he said. "We met around the tip of a big ledge. He arched his back and hissed like a big cat. Then he showed the wickedest teeth I've ever seen. For a minute I didn't know what was going to happen.

"Then he turned and ran. He had a long, looping run, like a big weasel. I measured the tracks—nearly five feet between bounds. He was really traveling."

No unwounded fisher has been known to attack a human. It would rather not fight a dog, either; but it seldom loses. Its curving claws are like those of a cat, but because it is not a member of the cat family, it cannot retract them. The claw-marks are good things to look for in a fisher track —those and the prints of five toes instead of the four shown in many animal tracks.

You'll seldom see more than one fisher at a time—if, indeed, you ever see one at all. Like its cousins, the mink, otter, and wolverine, it loves privacy. It claims a territory of several square miles as its own. Then it makes a regular circuit, traveling mostly by night. It visits the same spot perhaps once a week. It has regular signposts where it deposits a bit of musk from scent glands near the tail. If it comes across the scent of another fisher, it chases the intruder away. An Indian legend states that it was a far-ranging fisher that broke through the floor of heaven and first let the spring warmth out on a wintry world.

Once a year, in late winter, it relents of its nonconformist ways. The female goes to seek a mate. They may breed and part at once, or hunt together a few days before mating. She leaves him for a short time each day, for she already has a nest of young in a hollow tree and must nurse them periodically. If the male tries to accompany her, she savagely chases him away. She seems to know that he has little against eating his own kind.

In a few days they separate and she returns home, where the fertilized eggs in her body go through one of the strangest cycles known.

They develop a little and then come to a halt. All summer and fall they remain with no further change. Finally, in the winter, they finish their growth. Two to four kits are born just a few days before the spring mating season. So this Vermont resident has the longest gestation period of any North American mammal: nearly a full year.

The new babies are naked and blind. They stay in their den for nearly two months before they begin to travel with their mother, pouncing on mouse nests and sharing porcupines. Soon, though, they get cantankerous; and in the autumn they break away. If they meet again they fight like perfect strangers.

The thick fur of the fisher-cat, its slow birth rate, and its passion for solitude nearly spelled its doom in Vermont when man first came.

The pelts were magnificent, with fur so rich that it was quickly dubbed "American sable." A prime female coat brought two hundred dollars as recently as 1910-1920 (today fifteen dollars would be high). And since nearly every female killed was pregnant, with a little treehole family somewhere, the loss was compounded. Those that weren't killed retreated before the axe and the plow. At the beginning of this century they were at such a low ebb they were threatened with extinction.

Thus it was that, for the first time in history, the porcupine found its only natural enemy gone. It was quick to take advantage of the change. It spread so fast in Vermont that a bounty was put on its head in 1903. This bounty continued, off and on, for fifty years—and in 1953, the last bounty year, there were more porcupines than ever.

In desperation the Department of Forests and Parks made a study of the whole problem, and the 1957 legislature set up a control project. Shooting, trapping, repellants, and poisoning were tried.

"Over five thousand quill-pigs were killed· in the next two years," Ed Walker, assistant in charge of pest control, told me. "But there are lots of backwoods areas that

---

Some Fisher Facts

Eight to twelve pounds, so slim he can enter a hole five inches wide, the fisher-cat can leap forty feet from tree to tree, outmaneuver a squirrel; an agile and tireless runner, he can easily catch a rabbit.

The fisher is fearsome in combat, able to outfight raccoon and lynx, and even dogs if cornered or with its young. It may take sick or weak deer, too. It is thought to eat some nuts and berries in the fall during its usually nocturnal foraging.

Although not a water animal, it can swim adequately. It is shy but often vocal: one call being reported as "like a mournful child's cry"; or as uttering short, sharp whistles, and sometimes low grunts.

are hard to get to with guns or poison. And these are ideal fisher territory. So we looked into the possibility of releasing a few in such areas.

"Besides," he continued, "natural control is better than costly artificial measures. There was a time when the porcupine lived in harmony with the forest. He's as much a part of the Vermont scene as the deer or the sugar maple. We don't want to eradicate him—just put him back in his place."

I asked about the possibility of the fisher getting out of hand. What guarantee was there that it wouldn't start on squirrels and rabbits when it ran out of porcupines? What would stop it from becoming a nuisance, like the starling, the English sparrow, the rabbits in Australia?

"All these creatures were foreigners, introduced to a new land," Ed reminded me. "The fisher, on the other hand, is a native. He has always lived here. We're interested only in establishing normal numbers of the animal. In parts of the Adirondacks they have lots of fishers—perhaps as many as one per square mile. There's little porky trouble in these areas. And there don't seem to be any complaints about lack of rabbits in the Adirondacks."

The Department of Forests and Parks released about half a dozen fishers in 1959 and early 1960, mostly in the Appalachian Gap and Warren areas. Ed Walker pointed out that scarcely a year later is too early for concrete results with a creature so slow to multiply. But if the picture is the same as it is in Maine, New York, and a few other northern states where the fisher has been helped to return, a great natural balance will be restored: Up fisher—and down porcupine.

The "pekan," as the Indians called the fisher, has been protected in Vermont by law since the Thirties. But there's one other creature—unprotected by law—with

which it might be confused. This is the mysterious "black panther" of Vermont, whatever this may be. So a hunter, seeing a dark-furred creature stretched out along a limb, twitching its tail in cat (and fisher) fashion, might be tempted to bag a "panther."

Barring such mistakes, however, there's real hope that fortune has turned at last for the fisher. There have been signs of him already in 1960 in many parts of the state, including Barnard, Bethel, Concord, Halifax, Ripton, Searsburg, Starksboro, Westford and Williston. Soon, perhaps, he may return to his rightful inheritance.

The Porcupine

This forest-dwelling rodent, *Erithyzon dorsatum*, is sometimes locally called a hedgehog, although the true hedgehog is an unrelated European resident. He gnaws anything that smacks of salt. Campers are familiar with his taste for flooring, doors, tool handles, even aluminum utensils, cans and auto license plates. Having acquired a taste for synthetic rubber, the quill-pig now includes in his menu tires, tractor hydraulic lines, an occasional ski-lift tower pulley. He is reported to have nibbled dynamite.

Most animals give the porcupine a wide berth, so without control its population increases. However, his stuck-in quills are a hazard to unwary wildlife, dogs, people, and sometimes cows, which may nuzzle him when he visits barnyard or pasture.

In the forest of the northern half of our continent, porcupines are especially fond of the bark of living trees, often seriously wounding and deforming saplings and older trees alike. An individual can damage one hundred trees during a winter; in concentrations they strip young trees by the acre, often girdling and killing valuable timber species.

The Snowshoe Hare

RONALD ROOD

ROBERT CANDY Illustrations

WE WERE WALKING THROUGH A bunch of spruces and alders some years ago, old Charley and I. He'd seen some eighty winters, and I counted it a privilege to be tracking in the snow with him.

We crossed one trail after another of the tracks of an animal that must have leaped like a greyhound, doubling up so its hind feet hit the ground ahead of its front ones. The front tracks were the size of stamps, the hind ones like opened match-books.

Finally we paused. Tracks went up the trail, across the trail, everywhere but up a tree. "How many rabbits?" Charley asked.

"Well," I countered, "from the tracks, it looks as if there must have been half a dozen, at least."

Charley grinned. "You're about five rabbits too high." Then he softened a little. "Well, maybe it was two rabbits. But I'll bet there weren't any more. Old Snowshoe is a great hand to kick and run half the night.

"But he likes to do it alone. Snowshoe rabbits aren't too sociable with others—except in breeding season. Get more than one every few acres, and one of 'em will move off where it ain't so crowded."

This was my introduction to one of Vermont's most interesting woodland personalities. He's a critter that scampers through the woods most of the night and loafs all day. He wears a pair of snowshoes and boasts a set of ear trumpets. Neat as a cat about grooming himself, he yet rolls in the dust like a barnyard chicken. In spite of his nickname of "white rabbit" for his white winter coat, he's still confused with his little brown cousin, the cottontail rabbit, in summer. And, if you want to be technical, he's not even a rabbit at all.

Lepus americanus—the snowshoe hare—even begins his life, quite literally and figuratively, on the run. His mother seems scarcely to pause in her daily rounds to have her babies. She may give birth to them in a slight hollow or "form" kicked out at the base of a spruce or old stump—the only place she could call home—or she may merely have them at a sheltered spot along the trail.

Such a haphazard cradle would be a terrific handicap to most young animals. However, the little hares make the best of it. No naked, blind infancy for them. Fully furred, with wide eyes surveying the world from birth, they can hop almost at once. This factor separates the true hares from true rabbits with their helpless pink babies.

Several years after that winter's walk, I discovered a snowshoe's nest in June. It erupted in four different directions as the tiny family tried to escape my incautious gaze. Such bombshell behavior has probably saved at least part of a hare's brood from a pouncing fox.

At first the three or four youngsters stay close together. They're visited periodically by their mother, who transforms twigs, green shoots and leaves into her own milk for their first ten days of life. A young hare is an appealing little tyke. He weighs about

three ounces at the start, with half-short ears and half-long legs. His brownish-gray coat blends with the leaves—until one of those exuberant hops gives him away.

Within ten days after he is born the little snowshoe hare begins to sample the greenery firsthand. He begins an experimental nibble on a piece of grass or fern. Within a month he's on his own, trying out nearly every green plant that grows. His mother, meantime, is probably about ready to produce her second brood. She may have two families a year.

By the time he is five months old and adult in size, the hare shows another characteristic that's all his own. Last autumn a friend took me to a cage in his back yard.

"We hit this rabbit with the car last week," he said. "As soon as it's better, I'm going to let it go. But look at the length of those hind legs. That's not a regular cottontail rabbit, is it?"

I told him it was a snowshoe hare, for the long legs are another way in which you can tell a hare from a rabbit. In full flight, the long-legged hare can make great leaps of eight to ten feet at bursts of twenty-five miles per hour.

In September or October, the snowshoe hare gets ready for winter. Bit by bit the old brown coat begins to drop out. At the same time, hairs of a new white coat begin to take its place. Each fall on our strolls through the woodland we find Old Snowshoe in the act of switching garbs. The complete change takes about two months. Apparently it's triggered by a change in the length of daylight, for captive hares in windowed buildings will change their coats just like their wild brothers in the frosty air.

In full winter dress, the snowshoe is quite a sight—that is, if you can see him. His white fur blends with the snow perfectly. Only his dark eyes, twitching nose, and black eartips give him away. Pads of coarse hair have thickened on his feet so he can run on the fluffy snow without sinking. This, of course, is how he gets his name. So now, with boots and winter parka, he's ready for the worst that he can encounter in the way of weather—or in the form of animals or human beings.

And he seems to take delight in confounding them all. With many enemies, he may just quietly sneak beneath a snow-laden fir until danger is past. If routed out, he may run ahead a short distance and stop. But if his enemy is persistent, he jumps into the game with all four feet. Twisting and doubling through the familiar trails of his home territory, the snowshoe soon makes a hopeless maze of tracks. Then, as a neat final touch, he may circle around to where he was surprised in the first place.

One such race with a dog was witnessed by a friend with a pair of binoculars. "The dog was roaming a willow thicket across the valley," he told me. "He was just out for an afternoon stroll, when this snowshoe rabbit jumped up in front of him. That rabbit took off like a big white bouncing ball with the dog right behind.

"For a while he twisted through the bushes. This slowed the dog, but he kept right on the trail, barking his head off. So finally the rabbit pulled the neatest trick in the book. He ran right out into an old woods road. Then he raced down it while the dog was still nosing around in the bushes. He turned and raced right back in his own tracks for a couple of hundred feet. Then he gave a whopper of a jump into the bushes at the side of the road and 'froze' where he landed. You should have heard that dog change his tune after he'd run right past the rabbit and hit the dead-end where the tracks stopped in the middle of the road."

Old Snowshoe spends most of his life within perhaps six hundred feet of his birthplace in a wooded swamp or a bunch of bog spruces. If there's a country road near by, he may help himself to a dust bath now and then. He seems to have a liking for places where there's a little water, and can swim quite well when he wishes. But he's got just enough contrariness in his nature so that he won't always swim: stranded on a stump by rising spring floods, snowshoes have been known to starve rather than make a break for dry land.

With the coming of spring, the snowshoe hare begins to reconsider his view of others of his kind. Thumping his messages in a tattoo on the ground with those powerful feet, and straying across his own invisible boundary lines, he may visit the domain of other hares. There's lots of scurrying and thumping and fighting until the creatures are quite nearly "mad as a March hare." Somewhere in this progressive family reunion a brief alliance is formed between the sexes, and there's a new brood of leverets some thirty-six days later. The same thing may continue on into midspring for a second family.

Even in the exuberance of spring mating, the snowshoe hare must keep those great sound-scoop ears alert for enemies. But, in a way, his worst foe is himself.

Those Bugs Bunny teeth can get him into a lot of trouble. The incisors or cutting teeth are arranged with an extra set behind the first in the upper jaw, like a couple of spares. These teeth show his relationship to the rabbits and western pikas. They also point out his distinction from the true rodents, which lack this double row. The trouble is that, rodents or hares, the animals must keep gnawing to keep the teeth worn down. So everywhere he goes, the hare nips the ends of plants, leaving behind the peculiar slanted cuts which are the trademark of the buck-teeth set.

"They love willows," a forester told me, "and few people mind when they help themselves to willow shoots. But it's different when hares turn to maple or pine—especially when they're forced to it in years

of peak abundance."

He was referring to an approximately ten-year cycle of abundance followed by scarcity. "The hares build up year after year," he pointed out, "faster than their enemies seem to take care of them. They have a regular population explosion. I heard of a place in Ontario that was supposed to have thirty-five hundred snowshoe hares to the square mile.

"Then comes the crash. Almost all of them die out. Nobody knows the real cause. Perhaps it's disease, or parasites, or starvation or predators—or all of 'em."

We don't see this cycle plainly in Vermont, possibly because of the leveling effect of constant hunting pressure. But over much of the snowshoe's range—Canada, the northern tier of the United States, and south along the east and west mountain ranges—the cycle is striking.

Apparently the snowshoe hare gets along quite well, cycles and all. The Indians have long set snares in his runways. His remains have been found in the kitchen middens of the American mound-builders of centuries ago. And there are few predators—from eagles to owls to foxes to weasels—that would refuse a chance for a snowshoe meal.

But the snowshoe hare takes them all in his jackknife stride. He's still one of our most plentiful woodland creatures. Perhaps this is because he's wearing four rabbit's feet—just for luck.

35

Voice in the Swamp

RONALD ROOD: *On Spring Peepers*

MOST LIKELY YOU HAVE NEVER seen him. He is too shy and well camouflaged to attract notice, and he quietly disappears the moment you disturb his watery world. Yet he is such a lusty singer that spring in Vermont would not be the same without him.

Almost anywhere east of the Mississippi —from northern Florida and Louisiana to southern Ontario and Quebec—the spring peeper hails the change of the seasons. But even though millions have heard his call, to most he is just a voice in the marsh. Many have not the faintest idea what kind of a creature he may be.

This little frog—for that is what he is— begins to sound his first notes shortly after he comes from his winter hideout in the forest. Sometimes you can hear his high, piping one-note call up on a hillside, many feet from the nearest water. He works downhill as fast as the temperature of the strengthening days will let him, until finally he slips into the edge of an icy pool.

Soon he is joined by other males and the silent, egg-laden females. As their numbers increase, they seem to take courage from each other's company. The clear, upward-sliding notes, pitched nearly as high as a human can whistle, come with greater frequency. Finally, when spring is about a month old, his once-a-second calls begin to blend with those of his neighbors into a constant, swelling sound.

He is incredibly small for such a songster. Not a baby frog as many believe, but fully grown at one inch in length, he and his mate could fit comfortably within the bowl of a teaspoon. He weighs only a tenth of an ounce, but his voice is so clear that it can be heard nearly half a mile on a still night. If we could shout as loudly for our size, we could be heard about ten thousand miles away. The photograph of peepers on a pencil shows them life size.

This exuberant little midget is almost impossible to find during the day, for he is most active at night. And he is a master ventriloquist. The sound seems to come from nearly anywhere in the tangled vegetation. Then, as you come closer to pinpoint its source, he falls silent.

His leaf-brown back matches the color of dead grasses. Even from the point of view of a pickerel or pike, he must be hard to see, as his whitish-yellow underside blends with the light sky overhead.

The first time I saw this little fellow, one of the smallest frogs in America, I spotted him with the aid of a flashlight. Beneath the throat of the male is a thin distensible pouch which inflates with air as he sings, and serves as a resonance chamber, greatly amplifying the sound. The bubblelike, translucent sac caught the light, reflecting it like a single eye of some wild animal at the water's edge. It pulsated with each call, winking at me in the dark. (As shown in Karl H. Maslowski's photograph of a singing peeper, four times life size.)

He seemed not to mind the light, but kept singing while I crept to within a few inches. Then I discovered an astounding thing. That great volume of sound is not a song at all, but a hum. The spring peeper makes all his noise with his mouth closed.

A glance at his color pattern showed how aptly he is named: *Hyla crucifer,* the "wood nymph who bears a cross." Not only is he flecked with brown and tan like the twigs and leaves of the woods and bushes, but on his back is a dark cross. It is like an X, with the four corners at the shoulders and hips.

His eyes, like those of many toads and frogs, were things of startling beauty. Their jet-black pupils were slitted like those of a cat, but horizontally. Beyond the pupils, the eyes were flecked with liquid gold.

Each of his toes was tipped with a tiny suction disc, enabling him to cling halfway out of the water on a broken reed. So sure is the grip of these discs and so great the natural clinging power of the wet little body, that I have seen a peeper walk up the inside of a goldfish bowl and proceed, upside down, to negotiate the overhang of the rim, before reaching the edge and freedom.

Yet when it wants to, it can loosen the suction cups and leap three or four feet.

Soon after they reach the water in the spring, the little creatures begin to pair off. They frog-kick their way across open stretches of water between the hummocks. In their ardor, the males hopefully clamp on to nearly every floating object with their front legs. Sometimes two males, fumbling

AMERICAN MUSEUM OF NATURAL HISTORY

in the dusk, may meet and spar for a hold, evidently unaware of the mistaken identity. When one finally gets a double arm lock on the other, the outraged object of his affection kicks and thrashes until he is free.

Eventually the trial-and-error method brings results. Within a few days after he has announced his availability at the top of his lungs, the tiny swain has found his lady. She is about the same color, although slightly larger than her suitor, who hangs on, piggyback, with such a grip that it's a wonder she can breathe.

They swim around thus, in pairs, for several days. The male may continue his serenade right at her ear, to be answered from scores of throats in the water and along the shore. The volume of sound soon becomes so great that no individual voice can be heard.

Once I drove up to the edge of a swamp filled with spring peepers and blew the horn—long and loud. When I stopped, they were going as strong as ever. The little frogs, although gifted with perfectly good eardrums just behind those golden eyes,

took no notice at all. They seemed to be totally deafened by their own exultant chorus.

Yet, strangely enough, this riot of sound is their protection. Toss a stone into a swamp. At once, the peepers near the splash fall silent, warned, perhaps, by the shock-waves in the water. Then a widening circle of quiet spreads outward, like a swift-moving ripple. On and on it goes, until you are in the center of a shocking stillness. Each little songster, noting that his neighbor has stopped, does the same. Thus a swimming water snake or a hunting mink announces its progress by the bow waves of silence that precede it.

Within a few minutes, however, some bold little male tests the state of affairs with a single inquiring call. He is answered by others, and presently the song of spring is back over the swamp.

A few weeks after the first frog braves the chilly water, the eggs are produced. Aided in their release from the female by their own expanding pressure and the bear hug

of the male, they are emitted singly or in tiny clusters of six or eight. Pinhead size, they look like dark little plant seeds. They are fertilized as they emerge by the milt of the male, which is released into the water at the same time. There is no real physical union of the sexes.

The new parents separate as complete strangers shortly after egg-laying. They pay no attention to the freshly produced eggs. Yet so strong is their brief attachment that I have captured a mating pair and carried them half a mile in a sloshing bottle, still locked together.

The eggs cling to twigs and other under-water objects by their sticky gelatinous outer layer. They adhere singly, rather than in the familiar big jellylike masses that we know as "frog eggs." These latter are usually produced by larger species in the same swamp, such as the leopard frog. The eight or nine hundred eggs of each peeper may be as numerous, but they are seldom seen.

The babies hatch in about a week. Looking like rippling mites of black ribbon, they have delicate feathery gills. They hang motionless in the water, absorbing the attached yolk sac provided by nature to tide them over their first few hours. In several days they have turned into tadpoles a quarter-inch long. Then, with their rasping little mouths, they feed on the layer of algae and débris which covers their underwater pasture.

Now begins a dramatic race for life. In contrast to the clamor of the adults, who may still play in the water above them, it goes on in a desperate silence. Not only are hundreds of predatory insects and shore birds on the watch for the little morsels, but an even more ominous threat hangs over them. Many of the pools which were alive with peepers in April will be dry land by July. They must hurry through their complete babyhood in less than two months, or perish.

Often they lose by only a few days. Then the drying mud shows hundreds of dark gray spots to mark each tragedy. But a relenting nature has also given them a weapon against drought. If they are nearly ready to absorb their tails and transform into frogs when the pool begins to shrink, they are able to speed up their own development. The legs appear, the tail shortens and gives its substance back to the body for nourishment, and the undersized dwarfs, scarcely as large as a kernel of corn, make their escape a week or two early. Then they move to a puddle in the shelter of a hedgerow, and eventually to the coolness of the woods.

They must still hope for an occasional rain, however. Like all frogs, they must keep their skin moist or they shrivel and die. A few minutes in the hot sun will kill them.

This annual migration from the woods to our swamps and back again represents one of the oldest round trips on earth. It is far older than the migration of birds—older, even, than the birds themselves. It began when primitive fishlike amphibious forms first deserted the sheltering waters of the early world and tried a new life on land. As the ages passed, some were able to leave the open waters forever, ultimately giving rise to the reptiles, birds and mammals.

The amphibia, however, could not complete the change. Represented today by our frogs, toads, and salamanders, most of them are fated forever to return to the water for egg-laying and development. And so the little spring peeper still follows the racial trail made by some unknown pioneer back to the waters of perhaps 325 million years ago.

By June most of the peepers will have left the water. Then, from early summer to late fall, they hop through our forests and brushland, searching through the the leaves and low bushes for insects. I have found this little frog under stones in the deep woods. It's also been seen on the twig of a sugar maple forty feet in the air, from which it leapt fearlessly to land unharmed on the leaves below.

Often it is possible to hear the spring peeper's call in the woods every month of the year, for he may awaken during a winter thaw. Then he bravely pipes a few notes at the waning sun.

Usually, however, he sleeps right through the winter. He buries himself in forest humus or under a decaying log before the freeze of December. Then he remains in a torpor, his small cold-blooded body scarcely warmer than the soil about him.

Finally the sun swings north and the sap commences to flow in the maples. Then the cross-bearer comes to life again. Soon his welcome call from a thousand swamps tells us that spring's work has begun.

Spring

SONJA BULLATY and
ANGELO LOMEO:

An Essay in Black and White

40

Speckled Beauty

RONALD ROOD: *On the Brook Trout*

THE FIRST BROOK TROUT I CAN remember was a four-inch jewel named "Beauty." My father carefully lowered it into the rock-lined spring on our farm.

Day by day, Beauty snapped up the crickets and grasshoppers that sifted in around the cover from the meadow grass above. Every few days we'd lift the wooden hatch and dangle a worm from our fingers. Beauty would leap clear of the water for it.

Although we never learned its sex, we children kept believing that Beauty was a female and hoping that some day there would be eggs. She grew to be more than a foot long, and kept the cool waters of the spring free of insects. I shall never forget the pride with which I took a visitor from the city down to see "our secret," as we called her.

We lay on our stomachs, peering into the spring. I dropped in a grasshopper. There was a swirl of silver and color, and the 'hopper was gone.

When we got back to the house, my chum turned on the faucet. Drawing a glass of water, he presented it to his mother. Puzzled, she obliged with a swallow or two.

"Mother," he exulted in his new knowledge, "would you believe it? We just saw a *fish* swimming around in that water!"

After his startled parents had taken him back to their chlorinated safety, I received a dissertation on how not everybody was as fond of fish as I was.

Nevertheless I have yet to hear the first unfavorable comment about the brook trout. And by no means must you be a fisherman to admire the speckled beauty, either. Its gold and vermilion spotting and white-edged fins, the graceful fanning of its tail as it hovers against the current, its darting flight to cover or food, endear it to all who see. Even its scientific name has the music of a mountain stream: *Salvelinus fontinalis,* which means "living in springs."

The "brookie" or "squaretail" begins its life in the fall of the year. The female, laden with eggs, fights her way up the rapids and through the pools to the smaller streams. If she is a five- or six-incher breeding for the first time, she may work to a tiny brook scarcely wider than the pages of this book. Even if she is a two-pounder capable of holding her own in the waters of a lake, she still must visit the streams for breeding, or find an upwelling spring in the lake bottom. Otherwise, her race perishes with her.

Three of us of the Vergennes Forest and Field Club were lucky enough to see a female whipping out her nest one October. She had picked out a spot where a spring bubbled up through the sand and gravel of the brook. Darting upstream, she turned on her side and spatted the sand with that straight-edged tail. We gasped at the full beauty of her dark back with its convoluted markings, her blue-bordered spots, and yellowish underparts. Again and again she did this, while her salmon-bellied mate hovered near by. Together, they would chase away all intruders.

After several hours in the woods, we returned to the same spot. She was still at it, beating out a cavity, or "redd," which seemed to be over a foot in diameter and about four inches deep.

Soon, we knew, it would be cleared to her satisfaction. Then she would lay her eggs. Her mate, pressing her against the bottom, would emit milt into the water at the same time, and the simple miracle of mating would be over. Swimming upstream again, she would sweep the gravel until it had tumbled over the buckshot-size eggs. Then, without a backward glance, she would leave them forever.

Some states have *upper* size limits on fish—whoppers beyond a certain size must be returned unharmed to the water. In spite of the anguished cries of fishermen, this practice may have its place with threatened species—which, fortunately, the brookie is not. For, the larger the fish, the more young it can generally be expected to produce. Our little trout, spawning for her first time, probably produced from fifty to two hundred and fifty eggs. The number may run many times that figure in five-pound "lunkers."

All winter long, beneath their blankets of snow, ice, water and gravel, the eggs develop at near-freezing temperatures. They hatch out at what would seem to be the most hazardous period in the streams: when the icy waters are apt to be swollen and raging from melted snow.

But nature has made a wonderful provision for their safety. It supplies each baby with a built-in survival kit. I recall brand-new fry I saw at the Salisbury hatchery. Each looked like a pair of eyes and a backbone on top of a grain of rice. The "rice" was the unabsorbed yolk, so heavy in comparison to the fish that the creature could not lift itself off the bottom of the hatchery tray.

In the wild, the tiny young remain, safely buried in their gravel nursery, for more than a month. Slowly they "haul anchor" by absorbing the yolk. Then, when the brook has subsided, they work their way out into the waters that will be their world.

It is a dangerous world, even for a semi-transparent youngster whose dappled spots match the sunlight on the pebbles. Water insects snap it up; amphibians and even larger members of its kind are quick to seize it.

But the greatest tragedy of all knows no regard for camouflage. This is the result of the brook trout's constant need for oxygen. Let the concentration of this gas in the water fall below a critical level, and whole populations of brookies die in a few days. Or let the water warm much beyond the 70's and the same thing happens. Sometimes this is the result of "clear-cut" logging which removes forest shade, dumps silt into the stream, and sets up the stage for continued silting through erosion. The axe and chainsaw—if used unwisely in wholesale deforestation—take a lot of trout.

Each year our state stocks thousands of brookies (and browns and rainbows, too) in response to the clamor from fishermen. But few remain long, except in lakes—and even here spawning grounds may be poor, or competition from other fish may be high. Trout released in streams are almost always wasted if not caught. The native trout already in the streams are more than capable of populating every available nook all by themselves.

The key to more trout, of course, lies in that word "available." This I saw during a

WILLIAM J. SCHALDACH

walk along a pasture brook with a friend. Both sides of the stream had been fenced to keep cattle from grazing along its edges.

"Before I fenced this off," he told me, "this stream would shrink to a few scattered pools in the summer. Each spring the trout worked up into it from the river down in the valley, but they died off in August. Now that it's shaded, it keeps running. And the bugs that drop into the water from the bushes are natural trout food."

We crossed on some rocks placed in a line across the brook. "I put those rocks in to break up a long stretch of shallows," he said. "Now the water backs up behind them. And see that area just below, where it has scooped out a hole in the sand? There's usually a good fish there every spring."

Other parts of the stream had logs across them, with resulting trout-holes above and below. Here and there was a deflector of rocks to guide the stream against a bank, undercutting it enough for a trout lair.

"Ten years ago I had to count on the river to supply this brook with trout each year," he recalled. "Now, I almost think it's the other way around."

Under many stream conditions, trout will be about as large as your finger a year after hatching; hence the term "fingerlings." But growth varies tremendously. Hatchery-raised "yearlings," actually about eighteen months old, may be ten inches long, while their wild cousins may be less than six. Water temperature, food, disease and parasites all influence growth.

Theoretically, it's next to impossible to "fish out" even the smallest stream if you observe size limits. A legal-size brook trout (six inches in Vermont) has had the chance to spawn at least once, and therefore has left behind many potential replacements. But the fisherman who keeps undersized fish is condemning scores of trout unborn.

Once, while working on a stream survey

47

project, we made a study of trout food habits. As we suspected, the tiny fry fed on minute water insects and crustaceans. As they grew, so did the size of their food. Ten-inch specimens often gorge on caddis worms, those strange aquatic larvae which make a portable "shell" of sand grains or débris. Larger trout usually were found in the larger lakes and streams, where they took crustaceans and other fish, even including their own kind.

And the trout's appetite for hatching mayflies is so well known that a whole breed of purists—the dry-fly fishermen—has become established.

One result of our study came as a surprise. Norm, with whom I was working, called me over to his desk. "What do you make of this, Ron?" he asked.

We looked at what seemed to be black muck from the stomachs of two of the largest fish. Carefully separating it under a magnifier, we discovered it to be hundreds of tiny midges and aquatic insect larvae no larger than mosquitoes. How the sizable fish even managed to see such little specks, we couldn't understand. Big bait, big fish? Apparently not with these trout.

"But how do you bait your hook with a mosquito?" was Norm's comment.

In July 1916 Dr. W. J. Cook decided to try his luck on the Nipigon River in Ontario. The result made brook trout history. His fish—fourteen and one half pounds, thirty-four inches long—still holds the world's record. Our own state has kept no official tally of outsized fish. However, a brook trout much over two pounds usually makes the newspapers.

"We don't really know how large a brookie may grow," I was told at the fish hatchery, "nor how long it may live. But there's one thing we do know. It's not really a trout at all. It's a close relative of the trout and salmon, and is known as a charr. The teeth and skeleton are different."

Squaretail—native trout—brookie, or charr—regardless of its name, the speckled beauty is still the ultimate prize. Cautious, wary, sensitive to the shadow of a fishpole, game to the finish, it's a catch worthy of any angler. Few rewards are greater than the colors of a new-caught fish or the delicacy of its flesh, pink-white beneath the golden brown from the griddle.

Originally the brook trout was native to Canada and the northeastern part of the United States. Now it has been transplanted over half the suitable waters of the world. So kings can sample the princely fish that once only we could enjoy.

The best trout story I know came from an old account of fishing in the days before closed seasons had been established. While pointing out the need for protection of spawning fish, it also proves what most fishermen know—that the average fisherman has always been a good sport even before there were fishing laws.

"I was fishing in a little stream," says the fisherman, Eben Clark, "about the middle of October. I wanted a trout for breakfast, and hooked into a nice speckled one just as the sun rose.

"It was a good fish," Clark continued, "and it did not want to leave the water. Not only that, but it stirred up a surprising commotion. It swam as if it had two tails.

"Finally I swooped it up with my net. Then I understood. I had hooked a good female, loaded with eggs. Her mate had struggled right along at her side. He had followed every turn she made while she was fighting. And when I netted her, I got him too.

"I took one look at what I'd caught. 'I guess you two had better go back in the water,' I told them. So I let them go. And then I went back to a wonderful breakfast of milk and oatmeal."

The Washer with Restless Hands

RONALD ROOD: *On the Raccoon*

BENJAMIN E. ROGERS Photographs

THE NEXT TIME YOU MEET A RAC-coon, take another look. Chances are, he's up to something.

Of course he may be merely investigating a knothole in a fallen log, or trying to uncurl a dead leaf. If he runs across a closed garbage pail—even an empty one—or an old shoe, he will get to the bottom of these, too. For there's something about a mystery that's a challenge to a 'coon. He pokes that sensitive black snout in as far as it can go. Then maybe he reaches a couple of inches farther with a long pink tongue. Those teddy-bear ears cock forward for the slightest sound.

But his main information-getters are two little black paws. Tipped with curved sharp claws, they're like sensitive human hands of five slender fingers and no thumb.

Patting and feeling and poking constantly, those hands serve the raccoon almost like antennae. They sort through mud and soil, picking out earthworms, insects, and other delectables as if they were magnetized. They feel beneath the bark of trees, into the crevices of stones, or all over the bottom of a mud puddle. If a raccoon had a choice, he'd probably rather lose all his other senses than that of his ten probing little fingers.

We never knew how curious a 'coon could be until some friends gave us an adolescent one last spring. Apparently she had been abandoned near their suburban home, and I took her to release in our woods. For some reason, however, she preferred the vicinity of our old farmhouse. She has made her home in the eaves ever since—although she's free to depart at any time.

Nearly all of Scamper's waking hours are spent yielding to her consuming weakness —curiosity.

Put Scamper in your lap and she investigates the buttons on your shirt. Then she goes on to your wristwatch, your ring—or the inside of your palm if you cup your fingers loosely. First one little hand and then the other reaches in, exploring all around the inside of your closed fingers.

We give her dog food; yet even while she eats it, those hands are constantly feeling around in front of her, patting the earth, turning over pebbles. It's almost as if they had a will of their own and were completely detached from her, like the old cartoon of the pickpocket who pretends to read a newspaper on the bus while he's busy feeling for your wallet.

Naturally this curiosity can cause a lot of trouble. A friend of mine has a little woodland camp with a fireplace. "A raccoon must have got curious," he told me. "It climbed up the chimney and down into the fireplace. It tracked soot and dirt all over. It pulled out every cup and plate and took a healthy bite of a cake of soap. Then it pulled the sofa cushions off, probably looking for mice.

"It found a box of crackers and ate every one. It even licked up the crumbs. Then it batted a role of kitchen toweling the length of the cabin. Finally, when it was through, it slid a window open and pushed out through the screen."

But nothing's all bad. There was one redeeming factor. My friend had been using only one door of the cabin because the other one had a paper-wasp's nest in the eaves overhead. The raccoon, in climbing around the outside, found the nest and reduced it to soggy confetti. Raccoons are fond of grubs—even wasp grubs.

Probably it escaped most of the wasps because 'coons are nocturnal, and so the defenders were at a disadvantage. Anyway, that thick grizzled coat is almost perfectly insectproof. Sometimes a raccoon can be seen puttering around at the edge of a stream with a cloud of frustrated mosquitoes above it. They can scarcely penetrate that dense undercoat of fur beneath the coarse outer hairs.

The "black-masked little bear," as the Indians called it, begins its life in a hollow tree or stump. This may be a Canadian spruce, a Vermont maple or a southern palm, for raccoons range from Canada to Central America. In the South, a 'coon may share a few acres of home territory with its cousins the kinkajou, cacomistle and coati mundi. It's a cousin, too, of the Asiatic pandas.

Occasionally mother raccoon appropriates on old fox-den or rocky cave, but she seldom does any excavating herself. To employ those sensitive paws for such a purpose would be almost sacrilege. It would be like using a sterling spoon for a trowel.

Not that she couldn't dig it, however. 'Coons are astonishingly strong. There are few wild enemies that bother an adult raccoon. The same paws that can find a tadpole in the mud are husky enough to rip a belly open, and the white teeth are like those of a dog.

A logger told me of cutting down a raccoon tree by mistake one day in late May. "The baby raccoons were as helpless as kittens," he recalled, "and just about the same size. They were blind and hairless, but you could just see a hint of color where the dark band would run across their eyes when they got older. And you'd never guess they'd have bushy ringed tails some day, either. All they had was a little naked stub about the size of a match. We felt so sorry for them that we just left the tree where it fell. The mother stuck with 'em 'til they were big enough to leave the nest."

For the first month or more, the little raccoons stay right at home. Mother 'coon may remain with them during the day, but she leaves in the evening to search for food. When she departs, her family may go to the entrance of the hole to see her off. Down the tree she goes, headfirst like a squirrel, while three or four black-masked little faces watch her progress.

Sometime in June, curiosity gets the upper hand. Soon they're investigating the limbs and branches around the hole. At first they spread-eagle gingerly, clinging to the tree like the bark itself. Gradually they develop more confidence and finally make it to the ground. Then, if you're in the right place at dusk, you may see one of the most appealing sights in nature—a family of raccoons on its rounds.

Everything mother 'coon finds may be investigated by the whole family. The eggs of a ground-nesting bird or a patch of wild

strawberries will be kneaded and rolled between little hands and big until they're a gooey mess—and then the mess is cleaned up, for nothing is wasted. If they come across a turtle, they may spend half an hour trying to decipher it. But the object of their unflattering attention merely bides his time until some new discovery calls his audience away.

It's in a cornfield, however, that the raccoons are at their sparkling best. They like corn most in the milk stage—just when it's good eating for humans, too. And there stands a field of corn in the moonlight, with hundreds of tasty ears, all tantalizingly hidden beneath the husks. The family falls to the task as if it were starving—singly and collectively.

One ear is pulled down and the husks ripped off. But no sooner does the black-masked little burglar sample it than another ear shouts to be opened with the insistence of a candle calling to a moth. So the 'coon digs into this new one; and another, and another.

"If only they'd stick to a few cornstalks, it wouldn't be so bad," moaned a farmer as we surveyed the better part of two acres that had been ransacked. "But they've got to sample every stalk in the place. They ruin far more than they eat."

From watching our own little raccoon, I'd say that half the appeal of a cornfield is the fact that the ears are all tightly closed in their jackets. Perhaps some day the agricultural experiment stations will come up with huskless—and, therefore, at least partially, 'coonless—corn. Sounds impossible, perhaps, but it's probably easier than trying to breed the curiosity out of a raccoon.

All summer the family wanders around together, talking among themselves with purrings, whickers, whines, snuffings and little growls. Their front feet make little handprints while their flat hind feet leave a print like that of a tiny barefooted child.

If a tree is handy in time of danger, they scamper up it at the first suspicious noise. However, if a dog is unlucky enough to surprise them in a field, they can be formidable foes. And if they can carry the battle to a stream or pond, the raccoons are virtually unbeatable. Water is their second home.

This brings up a point which is often questioned: does *Procyon lotor,* whose scientific name means "the washer," always have to wash its food? Obviously not in a cornpatch, nor when it's up in a wild cherry tree, swallowing the fruit—pits and all. But if I give Scamper some dog biscuits or a few pieces of meat, she'll take them to a dish of water if it's handy. There she will

rub and souse and swish them around until they're thoroughly waterlogged. If water is not handy, though, she'll eat them dry.

Apparently the marvelous sensitivity of the raccoon's paws is heightened even more by being in water. Sometimes they seem almost to have taste buds in their fingers, so clever are they at feeling and finding edibles beneath the surface.

To discover the full reason behind "the washer's" actions you'd probably have to be a raccoon yourself. Whatever it is, it results in the improbable spectacle of a raccoon poking along the shore of a pond, snatching at a fish, and then solemnly "washing" the finny thing, even though the fish has been in water all its life!

By autumn the raccoon's unhurried ramblings and cosmopolitan appetite have resulted in his attaining practically adult size: some thirty inches long, perhaps, including a ten-inch tail, and weight of ten to twenty pounds. His fur comes into its prime—glossy and rich gray-brown, rippling with every step.

At about this time, too, a raccoon may putter away on his own, purring to himself as he leaves his relatives behind. Family ties are likely to become hazy as the time for winter sleep comes along.

Finally the warmth of day fails to penetrate enough into his snug den or hollow log, and he doesn't bother to come out for his evening rounds. His prodigious appetite has resulted in a layer of fat, so he just yawns and goes back to sleep. And there he will spend most of his time until mating season in March, coming out for an occasional ramble when it's warm, or for a raid on a garbage pail when his small stomach is pinched by hunger as spring approaches.

When Scamper began to disappear in preparation for her winter snooze, we investigated to find exactly where she was

sleeping. We discovered that she'd gained access to an unused portion of the attic. She had curled up in an old box of rags. There she made her little churring sound of recognition when I knelt beside her with my flashlight.

As I stroked her fur, she settled down and closed her eyes. Soon she seemed to be fast asleep. Then, just as I stood up to leave, a little black hand reached out from that ball of fur. Feeling around drowsily in the rags, it came across a button. Slowly, methodically, it stroked and twisted the button.

Even when it is half asleep, a raccoon is still a raccoon.

Natives and Newcomers

RONALD ROOD

GEORGE DALY Illustrations

OLD WILL WAS A RESIDENT AND stanch supporter of our little town of Lincoln. When asked if he'd traveled much beyond the confines of his beloved home place, he'd say:

"No, I haven't. And I don't aim to, neither. Couldn't see much any place else that ain't right here already."

Finally, however, some friends persuaded Will to go for a drive with them to Albany. As the car left the friendly little roads and buried itself in the mainstream of traffic, Will sat silent for a while. Then, pointing at the passing line of cars going in the other direction, he said, "See? What'd I tell you? Everybody's going to Lincoln!"

In a way, Will was right. For many of the plants and animals—just like the people—of neighboring areas have moved into the Vermont countryside. There they are absorbed into daily life until they become, in effect, Vermonters themselves.

Take an early autumn scene in the Green Mountain State. Cattle and horses graze deep in timothy or clover. Honeybees hum over the blue chickory and a few late-blooming dandelions. Corn grows golden in the sun, and pumpkins ripen on the vine.

A typical Vermont scene? Yes—and no. For, although you could duplicate this pic- ture in many sections of the state, not one of this assortment could be called a true Vermonter. They're all newcomers. Corn and pumpkins originally came from South America. The pasture plants were introduced from Europe, as were the domestic animals which graze among them, and the honeybees that pollinate them. In fact, the Indians had never even seen honeybees before and called them "white man's flies."

Even the famous Vermont rocks are largely newcomers. That is, if by "new" you mean a mere million or so years ago. This was roughly the time they invaded the land, pushed and hauled by a great ice sheet which crept down from the north. Since then, the ice has advanced and retreated three more times, wrenching great chunks from rock outcrops to the north and abandoning them here as what geologists might unkindly term "glacial garbage."

Just as the rocks are now part of the Green Mountain scene, many other visitors have made Vermont their home. It was November 9, 1894, that Vermont's state flower was chosen. After due consideration, the official choice was made. And so it is today that our state flower—the red clover—is itself a visitor, brought over by colonists and adopted by Vermont as her own.

54

Black Bear   Frog   Cotton Tail   Mink   Coon   Gray Squirrel

Intrigued by the thought of Vermonters-that-aren't, I presented the idea to the Vermont Fish and Game Department. "Most of our game animals are true natives," they told me, "with the exception of the pheasant, which is imported from the Orient. Oddly enough, the white-tail deer almost didn't remain in this category.

"Back at the beginning of the last century the deer was listed as practically extinct in the southern half of the state. The situation to the north wasn't a great deal better, either, for the deer does not do well in heavily forested areas. In fact, in 1878 the state actually imported seventeen deer and liberated them in Rutland County. This was an effort to save the dwindling deer population.

"However, with the abandonment of farms and their growth to underbrush, good deer territory became available. So we've been spared the embarrassment of having to import any more of an animal that was native in the first place."

The fisher, or fisher-cat, is another native that's had to be bolstered by restocking. Originally the fisher was a not uncommon Vermonter, and a sworn enemy of the porcupine. When fisher-fur prices skyrocketed, however, fishers got swift attention from trappers. This, plus other changes in living conditions, helped to lift the lid off the porcupine. Now, during the past decade, Vermont has found itself importing fishers from Maine to help bring the tree-chewing porky under control.

Beavers, too, have been moved into the state on occasion. Originally native here, they were scarce in many areas a generation ago, due to the effects of the fur market and man's tinkering with their habitat. In other places, their dam-building feats had made them a local nuisance. So they've been moved around by man, sometimes

White Tail Deer   Mud Turtle   Muskrat   Beaver   Red Fox

Woodcock   Gallinule   Ringneck   Bittern   Blue Wing Teal   Green Wing Teal   Ring Billed Gull

across town lines and sometimes across state lines, as lively pawns in a sort of giant chess game with nature. Wherever they've become re-established on land which was often rightfully theirs in the first place, they have been greeted with approval or anguish, depending on just what they've accomplished with their engineering feats.

Many of Vermont's birds and animals, of course, are in the non-game category. That noisy nuisance, the English sparrow, is a visitor who has come to stay. Introduced to our country in 1852, it was actually welcomed at first for "its cheerful chirrup," as one book put it. Finding many a meal in the undigested oats in horse droppings, it retreated before the advent of the automobile. "Sparrow killer!" the early bird-lovers used to shout at drivers of the horseless carriages.

Then there's the European starling. It's hard to believe that the first individuals were brought deliberately to this country in 1890; even harder to believe that they died out and were as deliberately re-introduced. Unfortunately they made it the second time—to the detriment of many less aggressive species such as the tree swallow and bluebird, whose nesting holes they often occupy.

There are other vistors to our Green Mountains that are far more welcome. "Ron," said Clifford Harris on the telephone one day, "there's a red bird with a pointed crest on my friend's feeding tray. It's the first one I've positively identified around Ferrisburg. I figured you might like to see it the next time you're out this way."

It was a cardinal—just like the dozens I've seen outside my window during an extended stay in Maryland. And since then cardinals have been known to nest as far north as Burlington.

Others which—like many human visitors —find that Vermont grows on them, include the turkey vulture and the whistling

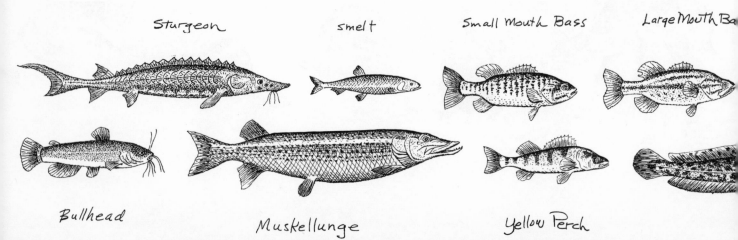

Sturgeon   smelt   Small Mouth Bass   Large Mouth Ba

Bullhead   Muskellunge   Yellow Perch

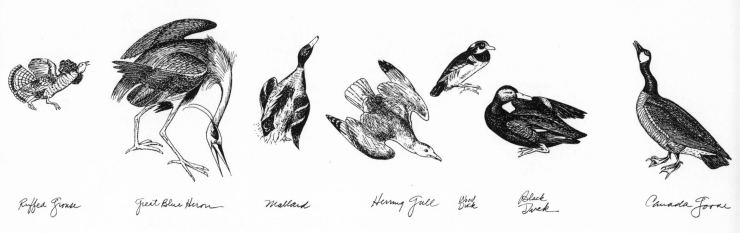

Ruffed Grouse   Great Blue Heron   Mallard   Herring Gull   Wood Duck   Black Duck   Canada Goose

swan, both reported from the Champlain Valley and southern Vermont. Even an occasional opossum, originally a migrant from Dixie, has come north for a Vermont visit. So have a few mockingbirds. And on a recent trip to Virginia I saw an insect which many Vermonters would recognize at once. This was a praying mantis, which is still another summer visitor that's taken up permanent Green Mountain residence.

Why do these creatures from "down-country" (general term for nearly any place outside of Vermont) become so successful away from home? Many scientists say that a warming trend in our hemisphere is helping creatures to extend their northern limits. Then, too, a bird or animal which moves to a new location may leave its natural enemies and diseases behind. Many of the starlings I've seen in Europe are quiet, well-behaved birds, as if they knew their place. They're quite a contrast to their raucous cousins in a land which has little de-

fense against their peskiness.

In the past twenty-odd years there have been increasing reports of another visitor—this time a Westerner come east. This is the coyote, of a strain apparently originating in the northern peninsula of Michigan and adjacent Canada. It has been seen on occasion in almost every part of Vermont by hunters, farmers, vacationists.

"These coyotes," a Fish and Game Department spokesman said, "will ordinarily breed with their own kind. However, in extending their range like this, they find a scarcity of suitable mates. So they breed with local dogs. Then you have an odd critter known as a coy-dog."

"How can you tell a coy-dog from a true coyote?" I asked.

"Well, true coyotes are usually white underneath, with buffy-gray sides and back. Their ears are big and alert, and they have what I call a 'keen look.' Coy-dogs, on the other hand, often show their mixed blood.

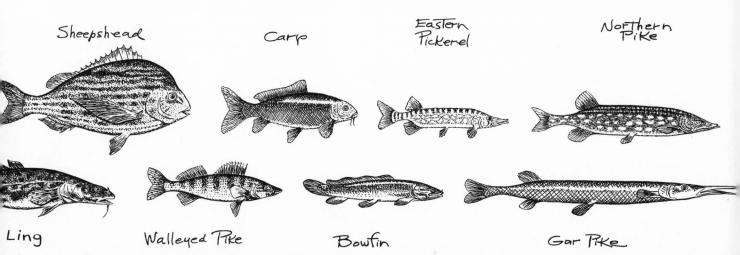

Sheepshead   Carp   Eastern Pickerel   Northern Pike

Ling   Walleyed Pike   Bowfin   Gar Pike

They may be any color. Their coats may be shaggy, their ears floppy, their tails curly. They're often somewhat bigger than coyotes, too—sometimes they'll weigh fifty pounds or more to the coyote's thirty."

"Do you think they'll become a threat to our wildlife?" I asked.

"Well, that's the big question. But so far, they've posed no great problem. They *do* chase deer. And they've been known to take grouse and rabbit. After all, they're predators. They'll eat mice, too. And berries and insects. The best we can say is that so far they've failed to live up to the dire predictions that have been made about them ever since the first one was killed in 1942."

Our waters, too, have their share of visitors. Fishermen angle for German brown trout and western rainbow trout in Vermont streams. They troll her cool waters for lake trout and landlocked salmon—which may have been introduced from the Great Lakes and the Maine area, respectively. They prize highly the silvery little smelt in Champlain and other lakes—actually a landlocked visitor from the ocean. It is alleged that a few lucky fishermen in the past have caught the handsome golden trout in the extreme northeastern part of our state—an import from Sunapee Lake in New Hampshire. Even the carp, esteemed as a food fish in Asia, has found Vermont waters to its liking.

There's another group that's on the other side of the picture. These are the creatures, once native to our state, which have now moved out. Some of them are known from old town reports; other go back to early records and stories told to the settlers by the Indians. They tell of animals we now associate with the Far West, creatures which were once Vermonters before there was a Vermont.

The American elk, or wapiti, was apparently once such a resident. It's quite possible that the American bison, or buffalo, also extended its range into what is now Vermont. Certainly it lived in the adjoining state of New York. Town records tell of wolves along the road in Lincoln not much more than a century ago. The legendary panther, or cougar, has gone to wilder parts, although reports still persist of this shadowy form in the Green Mountain woodlands. And the moose still occasionally wanders back to Vermont from Maine and Canada, like the old graduate who returns to his school for a reunion even though he's the last of his class.

Perhaps some of the most loyal Vermonters of all, the year-round birds, are mistaken for summer visitors. There also are the hosts of birds who visit our state each year to raise their babies. When fall arrives, they go south with their families. In the spring they return, faithful to their homeland.

Authorities are still not sure as to why birds migrate, but there's a strong feeling that their ancestors may have been living here when the glaciers came. They retreated to the south before the advancing ice, and their descendants followed it north again when they finally got the chance. If this is the case, then the annual tide of birds in its ebb and flow is perhaps a sort of racial "memory." It becomes active as the days get short in autumn, reverses itself with lengthening daylight in the spring.

And thus, if this theory does turn out to be true, the spring-and-autumn migration of the birds may be an indication of a family history which goes back even farther than the familiar rocks of the Green Mountains.

And that's old, even for a Vermonter.

The Esculent Morel

FRANK LIEBERMAN: *On Mushrooms*

ROBERT CANDY Illustration

INDEED ALMOST ANY MUSHROOM hunter will happily tell you of that one spot where he's always bagged his deer, or of the trout pool that's simply teeming with fish. He'll even take you to where he's found other rare and delicious mushrooms. But tell you where he's getting his morels this year? No, dear reader, that's asking too much, for the morel (*Morchella esculenta,* botanically speaking) is the mushroom

hunter's special delicacy and gourmet prize.

I don't mind telling you, however, that the morels used as models for the illustration on page 61 (shown about half life-size) were found in a Pomfret meadow. It's perfectly safe to tell you this now because they probably won't be there next year—morels are elusive!

My wife and a friend found this spot four years ago, and could hardly walk

---

Some Commonly Found Edible Mushrooms

Following are edible mushrooms quite common in Vermont, usually found in the conditions noted. The thumbnail descriptions are offered with the assumption that novice collectors, especially, always use a good guidebook to identify their finds.

PASTURE MUSHROOM (*Agaricus campestris),* commonest (and first cousin to cultivated supermarket type); open pastures; in September.

HORSE MUSHROOM (*Agaricus arvensis),* caps up to 10-inch diameter; like its close relative above, also in pastures (and likely near horse droppings); autumn.

INK CAP (*Coprinus micaceus*) has a self-descriptive name; at bases of old stumps, particularly on lawns; spring through growing season.

SHAGGY MANE (*Coprinus comatus),* white columns that appear overnight, on lawns; in autumn.

OYSTER MUSHROOM (*Pleurotis* sp.) looks like stacked oyster shells, grows on dying elms and maples; late fall till frost.

CHANTARELLE (*Cantharellus cibarius),* orange-yellow, funnel-shaped; June and July in rich woods.

GIANT PUFFBALL (*Lycoperdon giganteum*) is often as large as a basketball; pastures and lawns; in autumn. Like its smaller kin, discharges ripe spores in smoky clouds when tapped.

FAIRY CLUB or CORAL MUSHROOM (*Clavaria* sp.) has club-shaped branches, like coral; summer, especially after rains; in damp, shady woods.

in the meadow without trampling on morels. When we went back recently, we had a hard time finding enough specimens to make a showing. Morels exhaust their nutritional elements quickly, and when this happens they simply cannot grow.

Elusive though they are, it is more than worth the effort of finding morels, because they *are* delicious. Not only that, they are perfectly safe, for all morels are edible and easy to recognize; and no other mushroom looks like a morel.

The plant, consisting of a cap and stem, grows from two to six or more inches tall.

The cap varies slightly in form according to the species, and looks for all the world like a coarse sponge. It ranges in color from grayish brown to ocher yellow. It is distinguished by a series of broad, irregular pits, separated from each other by a network of ridges which are usually lighter in color than the pits.

The stem is thick in proportion to the cap, very pale tan in color, and both stem and cap are hollow.

Morels appear in the spring, usually late in May in Pomfret; and as to their habitat, let me quote from Captain Charles McIlvaine, the redoubtable author of *One Thousand American Fungi:*

"The Morel loves old apple orchards probably because ashes have been spread about the trees. Ashes and cinders are its choice fertilizers. . . . Mr. Moore of San Francisco says, 'We find it in profusion on burnt hillsides all along the Pacific Coast.'

"But it does not confine its habitat to burned surfaces. It grows in thin open woods or on borders of woods. It grows under pine, ash, oaks and other trees. Strange to say it grows under the walnut tree where very few fungi of any kind grow. Especially does it love the white walnut or butternut."

And true enough, it is under butternut

that I have been most successful in finding morels in Vermont.

One more hint: in the autumn 1963 issue of the Massachusetts Audubon Society's magazine, Nathan George Horwitt writes that he has noted a definite relationship between morels and elms dying of Dutch elm disease. According to Mr. Horwitt, a crop of five pounds of these mushrooms around the base of a single tree is fairly common, but he also notes that the next year there will be few or no signs of morels whatever.

Morels, along with other fungi, have been a choice article of food from very early times. From the writings of Theophrastus, who lived in the third century B.C., we learn that mushrooms were highly esteemed by the Greeks, and that there was a brisk import trade in mushrooms from Italy—Greece being then, as now, poor in fungi.

Among the Romans, mushrooms, including morels, were great favorites at the table. Cicero, in the first century B.C., wrote to his friend Galen of "elegant eaters preparing their fungi with such highly seasoned condiments that it is impossible to conceive of anything more delicious." Somewhat less enthusiastically, almost a hundred years later the philosopher Seneca wrote, "For they are not food, serving only to tickle the appetite, constraining those that are full to eat more."

However, along with good flavor morels, like other mushrooms, also have a modest vitamin and mineral content.

Because of their pitted surface morels should be thoroughly washed before being cooked. Then prepare them as you would other mushrooms. They are delicious simply sautéed in butter or made into a garnishing sauce for a steak.

If you're lucky enough to find a number of really big ones I suggest that after wash-

60

ing them you cut them in half, and stuff them with a mixture of minced ham and chicken, seasoned with fresh tarragon, if possible. Bake them in a medium-hot oven until the morels are tender to the fork, and serve with a Hollandaise sauce to which a touch of sherry has been added.

Need I add, "Bon appétit"?

61

Wildlife of The Lake

MILFORD K. SMITH: *On Champlain's Inhabitants*

BULLATY-LOMEO Photographs

IT WAS SAMUEL DE CHAMPLAIN, himself, who left the first written record of the fish and game life of the region that now bears his name. His *Journal* of 1609 tells of "stags, fallow deer, fawns, roebucks, bears" and other animals. The only Champlain fish which he noted was the gar pike. He described it as being some five feet in length, with a "bill" extending an additional two and a half feet from its head. The bill of the gar pike, he notes, when touched to the skull of a headache sufferer, was believed by his Indian guides to effect a sure cure.

Nobody else from that time to this has seen a gar pike much over three feet in length, including the bill. This, plus the fact Champlain also reported snow on the Green Mountains (in July), has led some historians to view the explorer as a truth-stretcher. Most sportsmen, however, believe Champlain was the lake's first white fisherman, and thus his description of the gar pike was merely under the license granted to all fishermen in telling of the size of the one that got away.

In any event there can be no doubt that the Champlain country in the early days was a fish and game paradise. In 1749 the indefatigable Swedish traveler Peter Kalm visited the French fort at Crown Point. "The lake close by," he states, "is full of fish and the woods abound with birds and animals. Those who choose to be diligent may live extremely well, and very grand in regard to food."

When the French wars were over and the first English settlers made their clearings on both shores of the lake, they were dependent upon the fish in Champlain's waters, and game in the nearby forests, for their sustenance. Atlantic salmon that came in by way of the St. Lawrence and Richelieu rivers were so numerous that settlers netted them by the wagonload at the mouths of the rivers that entered the lake. Many were dried and salted for future use. So common and monotonous was this diet of Champlain salmon that laws were passed in some northern New York communities forbidding the feeding of this fish more than a specified number of times to apprentices and "bound out" servants.

More dense even than the salmon was the flight of the passenger pigeons. By uncounted thousands they settled in the great groves of chestnut and oak. Pigeon-hunting in those days was more a slaughter than a hunt. They were netted and trapped and their nests destroyed. Like the salmon they were salted down by the barrel for future use, or for barter or sale. In many Vermont towns the "bound out" boys and girls became as tired of pigeon pie as did their

Heron and ducks

New York contemporaries of salmon.

The pigeons continued to darken the skies for many years despite this wholesale slaughter until, like the chestnut tree on which they fed, they vanished from the Champlain country forever.

The fall and the spring found wildfowl by the thousands winging along Lake Champlain. The pioneer would wait patiently until a packed flight of ducks or geese came within range of his heavily loaded flintlock. Aiming at the very center of the flying mass, he often could pick up a

hundred duck dinners when the cloud of black smoke lifted. An occasional wild turkey from the chestnut groves would provide a welcome change of diet. The ruffed grouse or "pa'tridge" could be knocked off a limb by a boy with a stick— a statement hard to accept by today's hunter who knows the grouse as the wariest game bird of all.

But with the bounty of the forest there were hazards as well. Bear, lynx, wolf and the dreaded catamount or panther prowled about the new clearings. Stray cows or colts quickly became their prey. Settlers themselves were not exempt from attack by these beasts. Almost any of the old Champlain towns has its legend of the lone hunter pursued by a wolf pack, or of a great bear attempting to enter a log cabin.

Equally dreaded on the new frontier was the rattlesnake, ruthlessly exterminated and now almost unknown in the Champlain valley. Liberal bounties and organized hunts by whole townships spelled the end of the wolf and the panther. The bear has now retreated to the fastness of the Adirondacks and the Green Mountains, where constant hunting has made him among the shyest of animals.

It is only fair to add, however, that there are those who will disagree on the extinction of the panther. We will not quarrel with those who are panther believers. We would as soon deny the existence of the Champlain sea serpent.

But whether or not Champlain contains a serpent there can be no doubt it does contain about as wide a variety of fish as can be found in any body of water. The salmon have gone, although a few of the landlocked variety are taken every season.

The biggest fish in Champlain waters, yet rarely seen, is the sturgeon. Growing to a length of six feet and often weighing more than two hundred pounds, it lives on

Muskrat house

the bottom of the lake. It feeds with a mouth like a vacuum cleaner on both small plant and animal life at the muddy bottom. The sturgeon has been said to reach an age of more than fifty years.

Not growing to the size of the sturgeon (thirty-six pounds is big) but a game fish of sheer savagery, is the muskellunge. Although comparatively rare it is found in the northern part of the lake. Akin to the muskellunge both in family and savagery is the northern pike. This wolf of the fresh water is distributed from one end of the lake to the other, favoring shallow, weedy water more than the clear depths. The northern pike may reach twenty pounds in weight. He will grab minnow, frog, young muskrat or duckling with fierce impartiality.

The southern part of Champlain, with its sloughlike rivers, also contains that chain-marked relative of the northern pike, the eastern pickerel. This lurker in the weeds is sudden death for small perch and venturesome frogs.

In these same weed waters, south of the Crown Point bridge, lurks the bowfin, an archaic sort of fish looking just like his fossil ancestors of Mesozoic time. He has a large, flat head, small beady eyes and a pikelike body; weighs up to a dozen pounds; will tackle anything that comes along, and even out of water is very tenacious of life.

As a table fish the bowfin leaves something to be desired. The ancient recipe for cooking bowfin is to split the fish and nail each side to a plank. The plank is then placed in front of a very hot fire and the bowfin allowed to cook for four hours. Then the bowfin is removed from the plank. After that, the recipe states, throw the bowfin as far away as possible and eat the plank.

65

Neighbors of the bowfin in the same waters are the carp and the gar pike. The carp is a foreign importation detested by most anglers, although a stout fighter. He is a long-lived fish of the sucker family and may attain a weight of thirty pounds. He often can be traced by the muddy trail he leaves, rooting like a pig along the bottom.

The gar pike, another of Champlain's archaic fish (with an ancestry of 45 million years), is equipped with sharp teeth which raise hob with smaller fish. In spring, when spawning, the large dorsal fin protrudes above the water like that of a sailfish. Its very hard scales have peg and socket joints, thus allowing them to be moved separately. This fish has no food value.

Two of the most sought-after game fish in Champlain are the two kinds of bass and the walleyed pike. The largemouth or Oswego bass inhabits the shallower or more weedy waters of the lake, while the bronze-colored smallmouth likes the clear, deep waters of the deep reefs and rocky shores.

Champlain Valley Flora

The Champlain Valley climate, like that of the Lower Connecticut River area, is milder than the rest of Vermont. This factor and the alluvial soil determine the flora native to the area.

This was white pine country until the great stands were cut back; typical valley trees now are red cedar, white and pitch pines, and such transition hardwoods as ash, basswood and oak.

Perhaps one thousand different species of flowering plants are found: many grasses and sedges, roses, clovers, lady-slippers and other orchids, cowslips, trillium, hepaticas, anemones, buttercups. A wide variety of interesting ferns favor the limestone outcroppings of the valley.

The walleyed pike, properly known as the pike perch, is found from the Canadian border to the Whitehall locks. With his protruding, almost luminous eyes he's hardly a beauty winner among fish, but he is the best of table fish.

Undoubtedly the most fished-for inhabitant of the lake is the yellow perch, prevalent everywhere in Champlain waters. These perch travel in schools and the fish in a given school are apt to be of almost identical size.

Equal in numbers, perhaps, to the perch, but found only in the deep waters, is the smelt—small in size, silvery in color and with a cucumber-like odor. Its ancestors were landlocked in Champlain when it became a lake.

In the deepest water is the ling, a fish that seems to be covered with flesh rather than skin or scales, comes equipped with strong teeth, and may weigh several pounds. The ling is a member of the codfish family and is another of Champlain's primitive survivors. It is listed as a fine food fish, but Champlain fishermen consider it a nuisance.

Members of the sunfish family are found in the shallow parts of the lake. These include the pumpkin seeds, blue-gills, strawberry bass, and even crappies. Sheepshead, another descendant of ocean-going fish, are found generally throughout the lake. They are fine fighters but worthless for food.

In southern Champlain's muddy waters and in the various "slangs" and slow-moving creeks which enter that part of the lake, dwell the ugly but toothsome bullheads and catfish. The bullheads, or "horned pout," rarely measure over a foot in length, whiskers and all. But the evil-looking catfish may grow to twice that length and attain a weight of twenty pounds.

Lake trout are not as numerous as in the

Canada geese

years when they were fished commercially. But they are found occasionally, as are their cousins the rainbow, brown and brook trout.

Wild ducks and occasional Canada geese follow their ancient sky trails in the fall migrations. Black ducks and mallards, wood ducks and an occasional teal all raise their families on Champlain. A dozen other varieties join them in the autumn.

The ruffed grouse or partridge still thrives in the abandoned apple orchards and the cedar thickets along Champlain's shores. And that hardy and bright-colored importation, the pheasant, may nest on the edge of the same marsh where the black ducks raise their young.

Raccoons prowl the shorelines at night in search of crawfish and frogs, with the sly and sinewy mink a rival for the same tidbits. Lake Champlain, which was the home of seals as late as 1821, also is likely to be fox country. Both the red and the gray varieties hunt the margins of the marshes.

These same marshes, in the West Haven and Benson sections of Vermont, are the homes of thousands of those sturdy little

fur bearers, the muskrats. Across these wetlands on spring nights, the big, green frogs boom their bass chorus.

One of the more familiar animals, the gray squirrel adds a tragic note to the Champlain story. Once in a decade or so the beeches, oaks and butternuts of the Vermont woods fail to produce any nuts. Then the squirrels start a westward migration. Although they are not the best of swimmers, they do not hesitate to venture the crossing of the lake, even in the roughest water. In such years the wanderer along the shores will find the wet, furry bodies of scores of these little rodents that have failed to gain the crossing.

Users of both the shore and water are the turtles of Lake Champlain. They range from huge, moss-covered snappers to the small and harmless mud turtles. Unknown in many waters but relatively common in Champlain is the soft-shelled turtle—fast and powerful and capable of catching a swimming fish. Sometimes in the spring, when the waters are high and muddy in the southern part of Champlain, a whole flotilla of huge turtles may be encountered on the lake, presumably on their way to

67

some sandy beach to lay their eggs.

The gulls have used Champlain for centuries. These scavengers of the lake patrol its waters from end to end and follow the tributary rivers back almost to their sources in the far-off mountains. On The Four Brothers islands, far out in the "broad lake," they nest and raise their young, with great herons and wild ducks for feathered company.

The wildlife of Champlain, whether in its waters, upon its rugged shores or flying in the sky above it, is varied and most colorful. The happy fishing and hunting grounds of the ancient Indians have remained today the same for the nature-lover, hunter and angler. Some of the fish, fowl and animals of Champlain have vanished with the ages, but new species have come to replace them. And the wildlife explorer of tomorrow will still find this historic lake a fascinating world of nature.

CHAMPLAIN'S

MONSTER

Leon W. Dean

Somewhere under the caverned bluffs of Lake Champlain, if men are to believe their eyes and children their elders, dwells a gigantic lake serpent. No one attempts to explain its origin. We know only that its presence has been reported from Bulwagga Bay, where it made its initial appearance, to Alburg Tongue.

States a local newspaper account of 1871: "The 'What is it?' of Lake Champlain was again interviewed near Barber's Point . . . in full view of the passengers of the steamer *Curlew*."

A man fled in a rowboat from the creature's path some fifty years ago. Two ladies fishing near Malletts Bay in August 1948 had the summer tan scared off them when they spied the monster disporting in their vicinity. So recently as 1954 a Vermont high-school principal and three companions sighted the thing while boating between West Swanton and Alburg. At first they mistook it for a floating telephone pole. Then it began to move, and so did they.

For identification purposes, the creature is described as being from twenty to forty feet long, and capable of traveling at a speed that raises a bow wave like that of a fast-moving power boat. Sometimes its body bulks well out of the water. Further details are understandably lacking.

Doubters contend the object is possibly the reflection of light upon the water, a drifting substance, gamboling sturgeon, or waterfowl skittering over the surface. Some people have no faith in anything.

Editor's note: Reliable witnesses have reported large "sea" serpents in the lake for more than a century. An account several years later than Professor Dean's summer 1959 story adds the detail of a globular head. The monster has yet to be photographed—or to be disproved. The woodcut was made about 1880 for the *Swanton Courier* and printed at the height of the sea-serpent scare.

The Return of the Whatzit

RONALD ROOD: *On Woodcock*

ROBERT CANDY Illustrations

TAKE A MOTTLED BROWN BIRD A little larger than your fist. Give it a head too large for its body and eyes too big for its head. Set it on comical little legs that spraddle as it walks. As a finishing touch, add an astounding bill nearly three inches long, out of which issues a voice like a Bronx cheer. And you have what some people call a woodcock.

It's known by many other names, too. "Timber doodle," my forestry professor in Connecticut used to say, when we'd flush it out of an alder swamp. Down along the Gulf Coast where it spends its winters, it may also be known as bigheaded snipe, night partridge or "bigeyes."

In the southeastern quarter of Canada, which marks the limit of its summer range, it sometimes goes by the name of bogsnipe, Labrador twister, or whistler—this last alluding to the sound of the wings in flight.

The name that fits best, however, is one which sounds something less than complimentary until you learn of the woodcock's habits. One of these birds was brought to me. It had been stunned by a car. The motorist watched me stroke the rich brown plumage and gently feel the feathered shins for possible breaks. "What do those bogsuckers eat, anyway?" he asked.

The truth is that, far from being ridiculous in its makeup—except by human standards—the bogsucker is admirably built for the strange niche in which it lives. That long bill is wonderful for flipping over chips and dead leaves to expose beetles and other small insects. It's best suited, however, for the woodcock's main fare—earthworms by the hundreds.

If you think of earthworms and how they live, everything about the woodcock falls in place. Earthworms are scarce in evergreen woods. However, they are found in alder thickets and moist hardwood lowlands—and so, here you find the woodcock.

Earthworms often come to the surface of the ground at night to feed on decaying plant material; hence the woodcock's long, probing bill. This sensitive organ also has a flexible tip to the upper mandible. Thus, even when it's buried to the hilt in the ground, it can grasp a worm in a burrow. The large eyes are wonderful for night vision and the short legs allow it to be close to the ground for its feeding habits.

Even the pattering little feet have their place, according to ornithologists. "Ever notice how worms come out of the ground when it begins to rain?" one asked me. "The same thing happens when a woodcock is feeding. It stamps the ground quickly and lightly. Or sometimes it flutters its wings. This must feel like falling raindrops to the worms, for they obligingly come up within reach of the woodcock's bill."

Whether the bogsucker gets all its worms in this way or not, the fact is that it's amaz-

70

ingly successful in finding them. The prodigious appetite of young birds of many
species is well known, but this bird is a
heavy feeder even as an adult. It may put
away twice its own weight in earthworms in
a twenty-four-hour period. The ground
where it has been feeding may be dotted
with holes about the diameter of a pencil,

looking as if someone had peppered the
place with a scatter-gun.

The timber doodle's new year begins
sometime in March when it arrives from
the southern states. It finds a clearing about
the size of a tennis court in a swampy woodland, or takes a stand in an overgrown field.
Here the male sets up his outdoor audito-

71

rium. Then, at dawn or dusk, he indulges in one of nature's strangest love songs.

It starts with a little hiccup. This is followed by the call note. Charitably, nature writers often refer to this latter as a "nasal 'peent,' somewhat like the note of the nighthawk." However, to many people it definitely smacks of a good Bronx cheer.

The bird repeats the hiccup-cheer every five seconds or so. He struts like an elfin turkey, turning this way and that and throwing the head backwards with each "peent." This gives it a ventriloqual character, and you may almost stumble over the singer in your effort to locate the sound.

After a few minutes the second half of the performance begins. Springing into the air, the woodcock beats his way upward. The feathers of his wings whistle in a rising crescendo as he gains speed. Higher he goes in a spiral which may take him three hundred feet above his singing ground. Here he begins a series of ecstatic vocal chip-chip-chips and whistles which become more impassioned as he circles. Then there is a sudden silence.

Now the woodcock dives to earth. He planes downward in a zigzag plunge, uttering a twittering whistle as he falls. Then, if you've been standing in the same place as when you first saw him, he suddenly materializes at your feet. "Peent!" And the whole process is repeated.

Woodcock are quick to take advantage of new opportunities. A favorite singing ground for woodcock near my house is the little town dump, scuffed out of the woodland by a bulldozer. I can usually hear one any time from late March to June. If the moon is bright, the aerial song-and-dance may go on all night. Finally it gets results; the female arrives on the scene and nesting begins soon after.

Since the singing ground is a most conspicuous spot, what with the male strutting back and forth and taking off on his courtship flights, the female nests in a more sheltered place.

"Consider yourself fortunate if you ever find a woodcock nest," an ornithologist told me. "I've seen just two. In each case the female looked like the pattern of the dead leaves around her. They're so confident you can't see them that they sometimes let you reach down and stroke them on the nest.

"Sometimes they'll sit right through anything. I once heard of a photographer who came across a nesting bird in the dense shade. So he got an axe and hewed a couple of saplings out of the way. Then he set up his equipment, took some close-up pictures, and left—and the bird never moved."

The nest with its three to five pinkish-brown mottled eggs is just a handy depression in the earth. There's apparently no special nesting material provided. "Woodcock babies look like tiny baby chicks," my friend continued. "They hatch after three weeks' incubation. They can run around almost at once. They have funny little bills just like mamma's. If you come across them in the woods, you'd better look quick. They'll 'freeze' so still that they disappear in plain sight. Their freckled down blends perfectly with the forest floor."

Also, the male apparently has just one mate, "although I've heard of at least one case where there were two nesting females within a few hundred feet of a single male."

How the woodcock tell each other apart is a good question. To the human eye, females and males look alike—except for a possible slight difference in length of bill. If the bogsnipe has a bill just under three inches long, it's likely to be a female. If under two and a half inches, it may be a male. "In fact," says my woodcock expert, "scientists feel that strutting enables some birds to tell the difference between the

sexes. If two birds meet and one struts while the other doesn't, it's a case of boy meets girl."

One of the most persistent tales about the timber doodle is that it carries its young about from place to place. Experts disagree on this point, but it has been reported a number of times. Apparently the young nestle right beneath the mother's body and make their way between her feathered thighs. Then, when she is suddenly flushed off the ground, one or more of them may cling to her for a while.

Whether they land safely, or whether the whole procedure is intentional, is still a question. But the care of the mother for the young is well known. If an enemy is near, she utters a soft "chip" and they run beneath her body or freeze where they are. I've seen a wonderful home movie sequence of a female woodcock dragging an "injured" wing just out of hand's reach. She kept it up, leading the photographer farther and farther away from the babies.

By early November, the bogsucker takes off to sample the southern earthworms. Still partial to moonlight, it may migrate at night, its rounded wings whistling as it appears in silhouette against the moon. Sometimes it goes in small flocks, feeding by day and flying again at night.

Because the woodcock is a game bird that migrates, it is controlled by federal and state law. Here in Vermont a hunter can usually take them during the month of October. That is, if he can hit them: they fly like a rudderless jet.

Like many other creatures, the woodcock is not against taking the easy way when opportunity offers. I've heard of deer which spent much of their time in an alfalfa patch instead of eating coarser twigs of the forest. A squirrel at Gifford Woods State Park spends its time on a regular "beat," visiting the front ends of parked cars, picking off insects which have been hit in flight. Now even the independent timber doodle may be able to change its ways. This was hinted as I talked to the owner of one of our Vermont ski resorts.

"A couple of years back we installed a heated swimming pool," he told me. "We ran spring water through it, and heated the water. Some of the pool's overflow, plus that from the spring itself, went down the mountain. Naturally the ground didn't freeze where this water ran. There was a little green grass there all winter. There was a brown bird there, too—just as fat and happy as could be. Seemed to be all bill and no neck. Just a little larger than a bobwhite quail and it flew as though it was half crazy. Wonder what kind of bird it could have been?"

I'm not sure, of course. But knowing that woodcock have been seen on well-watered city lawns in a dry spell, and have probed for earthworms in the thawed ground above an underground heating pipe, I have my suspicions.

And if it comes again, I bet it turns out to be a woodcock. Independent as ever, of course, but just enough of a pioneer to swap that long trip south for steam-heated earthworms. It will get first pickings, too, on the singing grounds this spring.

73

A Walk in the Springtime Woods

ERNEST GAY

ERNEST GAY

WATCHING THE GRASS GROW OR the birds migrate has never been classified by the United States Department of Commerce as gainful spring employment except possibly when the watcher is a botanist with a scientific study in progress or a park naturalist making a migratory bird count. Since I am neither of these I have had to fight off the last vestiges of a Puritan heritage to enjoy watching the grass grow or the birds fly.

Of course one has to concern oneself with making payments on the house or buying the children's shoes, and this can disturb the tranquillity of spring-watching. But I still watch, and though some may question it, to me it is useful—as useful, say, as free speech. Aldo Leopold put it this way: "For us of the minority the opportunity to see geese is more important than television, and the chance to find a pasque-flower is a right as inalienable as free speech."

Certainly I enjoy watching a ball game on television or a musical at the movie house, but no matter how good any of them are they are still secondhand abstractions. For me the firsthand reality of watching the grass grow, the migrating of the birds or the birth of wildflowers is the free speech of the inner man who discovers his identity in nature.

The Commerce department still won't classify it as gainful employment, but I wonder if one's not better employed to be a part of the spring thrust and woodland stretch than one of the thousands of anonymous paper-shufflers in the city skyscrapers.

In Vermont one can smell the wild mint, hear the spring peepers, see the delicate warblers. And, most important of all, just

74

by being outdoors one veers away from abstract man and becomes a part of the mysterious rhythms of the exploding new growth and feels the true advent of spring.

Where I live in southern Vermont that advent can sometimes be capricious—displaying a lovely warm day, a red-wing blackbird and pussy willows in March, then quickly reverting to a swirling snowstorm and below-freezing temperatures in April. But by late April or early May at the latest, whether it be by fits and starts or a nice clean clear-through explosion, spring will be here.

The phoebes, who somehow arrive just a few days before the houseflies appear in the old hayloft, will be flicking their tails on the power lines; the cowbird clan mixed with grackles will be noisily hoarding the sunflower seeds at the feeding station. There still will be a few chickadees now and then, but in an almost direct winter ratio they show up less and less as the warm spring blooms.

The brook below the house runs over its banks. The "never failing spring" (which fails every summer) is now overflowing with a vengeance that looks eternal. Even man in his megalopolitan cubbyhole gets the fever. (Physiologists tell us that man actually does experience chemical changes in the spring.) For a short time most adults become childishly giddy, and enjoy that progressive recession known as spring fever.

I get it too and walk about trying to "snatch each passing moment and examine it for signs of eternity." Signs like:

The gray and furry pussy willow searching for the warmth and light of the sun, as its ancestors have done for almost 100 million years;

The chestnut-sided warbler never staying in the same place long, a peripatetic bug-catcher flitting about with its systems always on Go;

The partially spun-out ferns at the base of the maple trees;

The pink bleeding hearts of the flower garden, lining up dutifully like colored chimes waiting to be gently rung;

The onomatopoeic towhee singing its sometimes thrushlike and sometimes buzzy operatic repertoire from the lower branches of a big-tooth aspen;

The swinging, bobbing goldfinch who sings on the wing;

A tasty-looking flowering almond whose round pink buds could easily be found in a Christmas candy stocking;

A few swallows sitting on separate wires, setting up a sheet of music;

A battalion of bloodroot wildflowers lending their petals to the light in a short display of early spring enthusiasm;

White-pantalooned apple trees on a green-pastured stage with a backdrop of deciduous props;

The life and death in a spring pond, where last year's drained gray leaves take their final swim among the vibrant red buds of this year's spring.

Finding these signals of spring is to my mind about the best employment Vermont can offer at this time of year. It's steady, colorful and varied work with great growth potential. Maybe we ought to have the Department of Commerce establish a "watch the grass grow" division. My guess is that it would take a lot of pressure off the health-and-welfare people.

Sociologists tell us that some day the government will pay our grandchildren to paint pictures or sculpt statues or write music or maybe even watch birds. That's wonderful for the grandchildren, but even if the gerontologists could figure out a way for me to be around to see it, I wouldn't wait. The pay is good enough for me right now.

DEER
MICE

RONALD ROOD:

On the White-footed

Harvesters

ROBERT CANDY

Illustrations

YOU'D BE SURPRISED AT HOW much personality can be packed into two small ounces. A deer mouse can sing and it can dance. It flees before the tiny shrew but it will stand up to a human being. In fact, if you've ever had any dealings with one, you know that it can be perfectly fascinating. Perfectly frustrating, too—but that depends on your point of view.

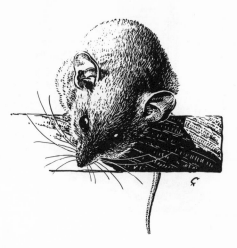

Take the fascinating side first. A friend of mine has a little cabin near my home. She comes up in summer for a week or two at a time. Last spring I was getting it ready for her, and as I poked around beneath the cabin, turning on the water and checking the pipes, I suddenly realized that I had company. Every turn of the wrench, every move of my hands was followed by two liquid-dark eyes, two alert, tissue-thin ears, and a twinkling set of nose whiskers attached to a brownish-gray body. And when I stopped for a moment the ears and whiskers poked right into where I'd been working.

Apparently fascinated by my activity, the deer mouse inspected my job like a little foreman. Finally, having given its approval, it settled back on its haunches. Now it began to groom itself with tongue and tiny pink feet, from its immaculate white underbelly to the tip of its long downy-furred tail.

Still marveling at the charm of the little creature, I went inside the cabin—and smack into the other side of the deer mouse's split personality. Unrolling the mattresses, I found that my friend had appropriated some of their stuffing for his own bedding. Thoughtfully, he'd made several holes in each mattress, no doubt to secure a fair sample of the contents.

Further investigation in a bureau drawer disclosed the musky-smelling nest itself, nearly as big as a flattened basketball, completely domed over and with an entrance hole near the top. Little caches of maple seeds and wild cherry pits, about half a cup each, decorated a pile of pillowcases and the back shelf of the linen closet.

I cleaned up the place, dumping a few dried blueberries out of an overshoe and sweeping up a myriad little "calling cards" left all over by the mouse and his family. I shook my head at a sweater that looked as if it had been attacked by a gigantic clothes moth. But, of course, when I went outside again to glare at the unwanted guest, he had quietly made himself scarce.

This is all completely in character for the deer mouse, or white-footed mouse, as it is sometimes called. Gifted with a marvelous curiosity, it investigates every inch of the few hundred square yards it calls home. It is far too high-strung to hibernate, and chooses a cozy place as a base for its winter activities—an abandoned bird's nest in a bush, the knothole of a fallen log, or the furniture of some lucky camp.

The mouse makes a nest of grass and shredded bark lined with the softest materials it can find, and it stocks the general vicinity with little troves of seeds, fruit, berries, and even insect pupae. Then, with evidence of its presence everywhere, it proceeds to disappear—unless you look for the nocturnal creature after dark or rout it

from its slumber by banging on the pipes as I did.

During the winter his activity may well be a solo undertaking, for the white-foot is not markedly sociable. It can't abide the presence of humans for long, and usually moves out when people move in. If mice happen onto a corn shock, however, a dozen or more may come to share in the bonanza.

With the ending of winter, life takes a different turn for the white-foot. The females stay coyly at home while the males search them out. As these mice may use the runways of other creatures and make few of their own, the quest may take a night or two. But when it's successful and the sexes meet, the female is automatically launched on a career that could hardly be equaled by the most enthusiastic rabbit.

Forgetting her shyness, she rough-and-tumbles with her mate in a whirlwind courtship. But the honeymoon is short-lived. In a few days, prompted by the already burgeoning young within her, the female enlists the male's help in making a new nest.

Finally, little more than three weeks after mating, it's time for the new brood to arrive. Philosophically, perhaps, the male leaves the nest. Often, however, it's to seek out the company of another female. The mother mouse stays behind with her new family duties.

Young mice are about as interesting as lumps of putty. Naked, blind, almost legless, they look like four or five pink little bees. They're on earth, apparently, for just one purpose—to consume as much milk as possible. Their toothless little mouths so fit their mother's nipples and hang on so tightly that a female frightened from her nest may flee with her babies still attached, banging along like little saddlebags. She doesn't run far, however. She's so well acquainted with her fifth of an acre of land that she has an emergency hole all picked out.

Of course a baby or two may drop off on such a jaunt, or she may have to flee without her young. But she's a fine little mother; at the first chance she comes back to pick up the strays.

A friend of mine frightened a female out of his beehive where she'd been helping herself to honey and beeswax all winter. His account gives a good look into mouse personality:

"One spring I was cleaning out my hives. I came to a big cluster of leaves and downy material at the bottom of one. It was the

78

nest of a white-footed mouse. As I yanked it apart, three little pink mice fell out. They were so tiny and naked they looked like little grubs. Then the mother ran out with a fourth one in her mouth.

"She ran over into the bushes and dropped the baby there. I held the other three in my hand.

" 'If you want 'em, you've got to come and get 'em,' I told her. Of course she couldn't understand me, but she came back to where the babies were squeaking in my hand. Then she sat up like a little squirrel and put her front paws together as if she were begging. So I opened my hand and let her take her little ones—one at a time."

The man looked at me a little sheepishly. "I suppose I should have killed them all on the spot," he said, "after all the trouble they caused. But when a little mouse shows that much courage, you have to be pretty low-down not to help her out."

In three weeks the young deer mice are weaned. By now the nest is soiled, and the mother may move to another home. Her family goes along with her, but their childhood is already coming to an end.

Within five or six weeks from the time they were born, they leave the nest. They pretty nearly have to—mother mouse is about to have her second litter.

There may be even a third family that spring. Then, for a whole month or so, the female may have a vacation from household duties. But in September she takes up where she left off in July. And by the time she has her last litter in October her first young-of-the-year may be having families of their own. Thus in just four or five months a female mouse may become a grandmother.

Obviously there has to be a damper somewhere on this white-footed little population explosion. Scarcity of food will hardly do it with a creature whose little yellow buck teeth will tackle anything from seeds to the deer's fallen antlers found in the woods. Water is no problem; the white-foot can make its own water chemically from the food it eats. Disease and parasites don't seem important, either. And weather isn't a factor, for deer mice are found from Canada to Mexico, east coast to west.

The terrible gantlet through which the deer mouse must scamper is the eager attention of almost every predator that

crawls, runs, flies or even swims. Hawks, owls and shrikes search for it from above. Foxes and bobcats pounce hopefully on grass clumps which may contain a nest. Snakes and weasels follow a female through the litter of forests and brushland until they come on the nest of helpless babies.

Once I watched a one-sided battle between a shrew and a white-foot. The mouse tried desperately to shake off her tiny enemy—for a shrew is scarcely as big as a mouse—but the chase lasted only a minute or two. One nip at the base of the skull, and the female collapsed. And at the same stroke some hidden mouselets were orphaned in an unknown nest of grass and milkweed down.

Most fishermen know that an imitation mouse is sure-fire for bass and pike. Even big trout have been found with mice in their stomachs. So whether the white-foot swims, runs about with its peculiar hopping gait, or merely stays at home, it is never more than a jump away from danger.

As though relenting for making it fair game for almost any animal, nature has given the white-foot an added protection—besides, of course, its wonderful facility with the multiplication table. If danger threatens, the tiny creature can drum a little tattoo with its front feet. This little dance sounds almost like the buzzing of a bee in the leaves. It helps to alert other mice in the vicinity.

There's another sound, one which I've heard just a few times—the song of the white-foot. Like a thin, birdlike trill, it's just within the upper limit of human hearing. Actually it is a succession of quick little squeaks. It has given the name "vesper mouse" to this little creature, which becomes active at dusk.

Research has now shown that the large ears of the vesper mouse can catch ultra-sonic squeaks such as those made by bats in their radar flight. So perhaps these mice can communicate in ways we haven't yet discovered.

Even science has succumbed a bit to the charm of the deer mice. Technically, there are several kinds, but two common sorts are *Peromyscus leucopus* ("the mouse with the white feet") and *Peromyscus maniculatus* ("with little gloves"). The Indians called it the harvester, or "quay-non-wit-wa-go-no-chi," a name almost as long as its six-inch body, half of which is tail. In fact, so impressed were the Indians with its industriousness in gathering winter stores that when they found a cache of beechnuts or edible beans, they were careful to replace the treasure, seed for seed, with maize.

Chances are that the mouse which runs across the sunlit road in front of you is *not* a white-foot. More likely, it's a field mouse or a pine mouse, for they are seen more frequently during the day. And the white-foot has a number of other rodent cousins, such as the graceful jumping mouse (with its astonishing six-foot leaps), and the muskrat which, technically, is a huge swimming mouse.

Although the white-foot is one of our most common woodland mammals, you may have to make a special effort to see it. Look for it with a flashlight after dark in the woods. Watch it run up and down a hazel bush, cutting the nuts and searching for them on the ground.

Or, of course, you could merely build a cabin in a woodland clearing, or buy an old Vermont farmhouse with overgrown weeds and bushes sneaking up on it. Then you may not have to search at all. In fact, until you make things too civilized, the soft-furred creature with the little gloves is likely to come to *you*.

Wildflowers of Spring

GEORGE D. AIKEN

CHARLES CLEVELAND JOHNSON

Color Portfolio

THREE HUNDRED YEARS AGO THE North American continent was an unknown wilderness, peopled by a primitive race and replete with an abundance of wild animal and plant life. Then, as the hardy and adventurous pioneers of the old world sought out our shores in great numbers, the native Americans—people, animals, and plants—were crowded back, slowly at first, but with ever increasing rapidity until now only a small fraction of their former number remains.

What a paradise of wildflowers the early pioneers must have found! And, looking at some of these flowers, I can see the pages of history turn backward and visualize those who gazed upon them for the first time.

In the Showy Ladyslipper, I see the Jesuits of France, their canoes breasting the currents of mighty rivers, as they plunge deeper and deeper into the forests to establish the outpost of civilization in the far-flung recesses of the vast Canadian wilderness. . . .

And the Hepaticas, Bloodroots, Violets and Columbine, in them is colonial New England—school days, homemade clothes and bare feet, the bunch of flowers shyly placed on the teacher's desk, childhood games, laughter and sorrow.

Yes, the wildflowers have seen the development of the comforts of our so-called civilization. They have seen the forest cut away, cities and villages grow up, roads made, bogs and marshes drained for agricultural purposes, great reservoirs built, flooding the fertile basins, and with each new development they have suffered.

Constantly pushed back by immigrant people, immigrant animals, and even immigrant plants, many species are now making a gallant last stand in the face of extermination.

In the farthest corner of my father's pasture was a small woodlot of sugar maples, birches, hop hornbeam and pig-

81

nut hickory, growing on rocky, ledgy ground. The cows were usually turned out to pasture the last of April, and it was my work and that of old Shep to get them down to the bars in time for milking every night. Usually their bovine obstinacy would prompt them to linger in this small woodlot in the far end of the pasture to make Shep and me as much work as possible in getting them. But in this little grove of hardwoods there were quantities of Spring Beauties, Hepaticas, Bloodroot, Violets, Squirrelcorn and Dutchmans-breeches, which so entranced the young man of eight years that it was occasionally necessary for some older member of the family to not only come after the cows, but Shep and me as well.

One night I dug and brought home a clump of Dutchmans-breeches and planted it under the lilac bush. I know now that blossoming time is not the proper time to move Dutchmans-breeches, but Providence looks after those who know no better, and that clump lived in its new home for nearly twenty years before the suckers of the lilac finally obliterated it. This was the first wild gardening I ever did.

It has been a good many years since I have been after the cows and listened to the silent but impressive sermons preached by Jack-in-the-pulpit or stained my face and hands with wild strawberries, but the friendly feeling for the wild things of the woods and fields which I acquired in those philosophical younger days has persisted. I always regarded the wildflowers of the woods as members of the family and rather felt it my duty to look after them as far as possible, while they in turn would impart many secrets which could never be learned inside the schoolhouse walls.

Great changes have taken place in our New England hills since I moved that clump of Dutchmans-breeches. Groves of great trees, under whose branches the dainty people of the woods lived and thrived, have been cut for lumber, and in their place is a maze of young growth so thick that only here and there are the wildflowers, formerly so abundant, able to survive. The open pastures are being covered with sapling growth of birches and pine not yet old enough to furnish shade and shelter for our woodland flowers, but just large enough to choke out the flowers of the open fields.

Even the people are changing. Formerly the hillside farms in New England were occupied by hard-working Yankee farmers, who struggled so industriously to wrest a living from the land that they had scant time to enjoy the beauties of the wildflowers. These farms are now being rapidly occupied by folks from the cities, good folks —most of them—but still folks who take such pride in the ownership of land in the country that they nail up "No trespassing" signs on every corner.

And then our roads. They are better, much better than we used to have, but this very fact has had disastrous results for many of our wildflower neighbors. Even from distant cities the automobile brings friends and relatives to the farmer's home on Sunday afternoon, and when they leave the back of the car may be laden with, besides tired human beings, masses of Laurel, Azaleas, Columbine or Arbutus, and our roadsides become so much poorer. I would not for an instant deny the people the right to enjoy and love our wildflowers, but the sad part of the story is that the loveliest wildflowers are being almost exterminated in the most accessible places.

What are we going to do about it? Well, some of us have spent a great many years thinking over this problem. Passing laws does not do any good, because with the permission of the landowner anyone may

82

gather wildflowers under the protection of the Constitution. Posting land on the part of the estate owners may preserve these plants, but where they may be enjoyed by comparatively few people.

I believe that all human people need close association with Nature's people. . . . Within recent years there have been established many wildflower preserves where the aim is to grow as many species as possible, so students and others who are unable to take long trips through the country may see them and study them. This work should be encouraged, for it not only provides a means by which our people may become acquainted with our wildflowers, but also, if properly taken care of, insures the perpetuation and source of seed supply of many rare and unusual varieties.

What a wonderful thing it would be if just outside every city or large town there could be established a wildflower preserve. People could be taught not only how to grow the plants, but also how to gather the flowers without injury to the future supply. They could learn how useless it is to try to transplant certain species into the wrong location or at the wrong time of the year. They could learn how to cut the blossoms of Azaleas and Mountain Laurel so that instead of being ruined the bushes would become thriftier and more free-blooming than ever; how Princess Pine may be gathered without doing the least harm, and so many other things they ought to know.

After all, Nature has given us the wild things to enjoy, and when we see children, or even grownups, thoughtlessly gathering flowers and plants because they have the natural human love for them, but which will result in disaster for the plants, isn't it better to explain to them the futility of what they are attempting and the resultant loss to everyone, than to berate them for their ignorance?

[The passages above, and the following descriptions of the flowers photographed by Mr. Johnson, are from *Pioneering with Wildflowers* by George D. Aiken, published by the author in 1933.]

Skunk Cabbage *(Symplocarpus foetidus)* must be of a sensitive nature. At any rate, it sends its large, curious, hooded brown flowers up so early in the spring that they are gone before their outrageous odor can be compared with the fragrance of other spring flowers. It is indeed a freak of Nature, presenting an almost tropical appearance at a time of year when snowbanks are still prevalent in the Northern woods.

Bloodroot *(Sanguinaria canadensis).* Its pure white blossoms on stems six to eight inches tall in April are very beautiful. The leaves of the Bloodroot are beautiful until late summer, when they die down.

Dutchmans-breeches *(Dicentra Cucullaria)* is very much at home on shelving rocks where the plant food of centuries has accumulated. After blossoming in April, the leaves stay green until June, when they die down.

Roundleaf Yellow Violet *(Viola rotundifolia)* is one of the earliest wildflowers to bloom, the tiny, bright yellow flowers on one- to three-inch stems blossoming while there is still snow in the woods.

Common Troutlily *(Erythronium americanum)* is quite commonly called Adderstongue or Dogtooth Violet. The leaves are much more beautiful than those of the White Troutlily, which is well, because it mats its bulbs so thickly that they have scarcely room to develop, and it blossoms much less frequently than its white relatives from the Central states.

Trailing Arbutus or **Mayflower** *(Epigaea repens)* blossoms in early May. It has one prime requirement: the soil must be very acid. It grows better in shade than in full sun.

Roundlobe Hepatica or **Liverleaf** *(Hepatica americana* or *triloba)*, while varying in color from white to dark blue, with occasional pinks, is more likely to be pale blue. It usually declines to grow in the same vicinity as its sharp-lobed relative, and chooses as its companions the Fringed Polygala, Moccasin Flower, Lowbush Blueberry and other plants requiring intensely acid soil.

Broadleaf Spring Beauty *(Claytonia caroliniana)*. Its dainty, pink-striped flowers blossom in early spring, growing from irregularly shaped bulbs which Nature plants two to three inches below the surface.

Wood Anemone or **Windflower** *(Anemone quinquefolia)*. I do not know how it got its name, but maybe because it is so fragile that it seems as if a strong wind might blow it away. The roots are threadlike and creeping, and in May the delicate white blossoms, about an inch broad, seem all out of proportion in size to the slender plant.

Sweet White Violet *(Viola blanda)* is usually found growing in moist woods and in bogs, and is a most beautiful little wildflower.

Canada Wild Ginger *(Asarum canadense)* creeps erratically along the ground as if it is not sure just where it is going, and hesitates every few inches to send up its large, downy, heart-shaped leaves. In April and May the reddish brown, bell-shaped flowers lie prostrate on the ground or sometimes buried in débris. The aromatic flavor of the root is responsible for its common name.

Jack-in-the-pulpit *(Arisaema triphyllum)* sometimes has a green pulpit, sometimes a striped green-and-brown one. Jack produces a cluster of brilliant red berries, which fall to the ground in early September and germinate so readily that the following year he may likely be surrounded by a numerous colony of little preachers.

Wild Sarsaparilla *(Aralia nudicaulis)*. The yellowish flowers of this plant of the roadside and woods are not conspicuous at blossoming time in May, but the large clusters of blue berries in late summer make it attractive.

Wild Dwarf Dogwood or **Bunchberry** *(Cornus canadensis)* spreads from creeping root stalks and forms a carpet in the moist woods where the soil is sufficiently acid. The flowers are pure white, and produced so freely as to form a sheet of white on the forest floor. The scarlet fruit ripens in late summer and is borne in bunches.

Painted Trillium *(Trillium undulatum)*, a late May bloomer, likes a different location from the rest of the family and insists on growing in very acid soil along with Bunchberry and Trailing Arbutus. Although the other trilliums have showy seed pods in August, the fruit of the Painted Trillium is the most striking of all, being intensely red and enlivening a dull season with its brilliant color.

Fringed Polygala or **Gaywings** *(Polygala paucifolia)*. The showy, dark pink blossoms are borne on four- to six-inch stems in late May and early June and, from the appearance of the flowers, might easily be mistaken for a small orchid, but of course they have nothing in common. It grows in rather dry soil under hardwoods or to a considerable extent under evergreens. Sometimes a pure white flowering plant is found.

SKUNK CABBAGE (*Symplocarpus foetidus*)

BLOODROOT (*Sanguinaria canadensis*)

DUTCHMANS-BREECHES (*Dicentra Cucullaria*)

ROUNDLEAF YELLOW VIOLET (*Viola rotundifolia*)

86

COMMON TROUTLILY or ADDERS-TONGUE (*Erythronium americanum*)

TRAILING ARBUTUS or MAYFLOWER (*Epigaea repens*)

ROUNDLOBE HEPATICA or LIVERLEAF (*Hepatica americana* or *triloba*)

BROADLEAF SPRING BEAUTY (*Claytonia caroliniana*)

WOOD ANEMONE or WINDFLOWER (*Anemone quinquefolia*)

SWEET WHITE VIOLET (*Viola blanda*)

89

CANADA WILD GINGER (*Asarum canadense*)

JACK-IN-THE-PULPIT (*Arisaema triphyllum*)

WILD SARSAPARILLA (*Aralia nudicaulis*)

WILD DWARF DOGWOOD or BUNCHBERRY (*Cornus canadensis*)

91

Painted Trillium (*Trillium undulatum*)

Fringed Polygala or Gaywings (*Polygala paucifolia*)

Cheerful Pacifist

RONALD ROOD: *On the Skunk*

ROBERT CANDY Illustration

AS A BOY I ALWAYS MANAGED TO stay clear of skunks. But my luck finally ran out five years ago.

I was going after the family cow with the kids and Jack, our shepherd dog. As we climbed a hill in the pasture, we could see Daisy munching grass down at the edge of a little gully.

Jack saw Daisy too, and bounded after her. But as he closed the distance between them we saw a motion in the gully. It was a skunk, hidden from the dog but right in his path.

I yelped a warning. Jack must have taken it for a round of applause, for he doubled his stride. With a joyous leap he launched himself over the edge of the gully.

About in mid-flight he discovered his mistake. He clawed the air with all fours but his momentum carried him on. Although he lit some three feet from the skunk in a running turn, this was far too close. In one smooth motion, the wood pussy came to attention, wheeled and fired.

Fortunately for Jack, the skunk wasn't too good as a snap shooter. The little cloud of spray missed its target.

Daisy, however, wasn't so lucky. We watched in fascination as the mist fanned out in the breeze and drifted toward her. In a moment she was enveloped in the fumes. Up went her head in surprise as she looked accusingly at the disappearing Jack.

The kids and I contemplated the scene, deeply impressed. Then Roger broke through my thoughts. "Do you still want the cow, Dad?"

I winced at the prospect of snuggling close to those fragrant flanks for the night's milking. But the task, of course, had to be done. When we finally got the discontented cow into the barn, we sponged her down with vinegar and tomato juice. Then her aroma wasn't nearly so bad. After a week we'd forgotten the whole affair—except on rainy days when the dampness brought Daisy's perfume out all over again. And the general area around the gully smelled in the rain, too.

The skunk, of course, had forgotten the encounter in ten seconds. This is the way with the little tyke. That tomcat-sized body with the plumed tail seems incapable of harboring a grudge. From pasture to suburbs to woodlot, life to a skunk is apparently one big peaceful round of crickets, beetles and the eggs of ground-nesting birds —punctuated occasionally by the spectacle of a bear or a bobcat backing respectfully away like a slave before an emperor.

I know few animals that will tangle with a skunk unless they're desperate. A direct hit with that smelly spray at close range can blind an animal for hours, or even permanently. It even burns when it comes in contact with the bare skin. Squeezed out of two little muscular glands beneath the tail, it amazingly contains only three or four drops broken into a fine mist. It can jet ten feet or more—lots more, if the wind is right. And the skunk can fire one or both barrels half a dozen times without reloading.

About the only creature that doesn't give a hoot about the smell is the great horned owl. Since he can grab with his taloned feet, he doesn't get the full blast of the skunk's weapon. Often a horned owl's nest reeks with the fumes. Needless to say the owl, like most other birds, has a poor sense of smell.

Ordinarily the skunk throws his tail well forward so as to be out of the way when he zeroes in on an enemy. He also is likely to shift his feet quickly so both ends of the body face the target—thus making himself into a letter U. From these observations, some people have concluded that a skunk lifted by his tail must be harmless.

"Well, they're not so handy at shooting in this position," was the way a game warden put it when I asked him about this, "so they often hold their fire. But this brings up an interesting question: once you've lifted a skunk off the ground, how do you put him down again?"

Skunks seldom use their weapon on each other. In fact, it's the rare skunk that smells at all. Many of them putter along nearsightedly through life without ever needing to defend themselves. After all, that warning pattern of black fur with the white V running backward from the nape of the neck is usually enough to change any enemy's mind.

Since skunk fur is seldom skunky, there has long been a brisk demand for the lustrous, coarse-haired pelt, although it's often marketed under such names as black marten or Alaska sable.

The smelly musk itself has long been used as a fixative for fine perfumes. And my grandmother used to keep a jar of oil tried out from skunk fat. "Good liniment and cold cure," she used to say.

Father skunk may view family ties with the same unconcern as he does everything else. In mid-February he begins his search for a mate. She may still be underground in her den, or the two may meet in a woodland clearing. Occasionally the tryst takes place under the porch of some lucky houseowner. Courtship often involves kittenish play and frolic, to the accompaniment of churrs and growls and chatterings.

Eventually, mating takes place. The two remain together for a few days, but then part company. The male goes his own way —"perhaps," as a lady biologist delicately informed me, "because it's still spring."

Now his flat-footed little five-pounder of a mate has her own duties to perform. She picks out an abandoned woodchuck burrow, perhaps, or enlarges a hollow under an old stump with her strong claws. Sometimes she merely fixes over her winter den. As her nine-week period draws to a close, she hauls in soft vegetation for her nest.

A boy who knew of my interest in wildlife took me to see five skunk kittens a couple of years ago. It was late April and they had obviously just been born. They'd been exposed when a shelving rock had been moved by a logging tractor.

We heard the nest even before we saw it. The skunklets made a chittering sound, like baby birds. They were black, wrinkled, toothless and blind, with about as much hair as a peach. Even so, the white striping

was visible, apparently ingrained in the skin.

I accidentally stepped on a twig and a piece of it fell on their nest. Instantly the chittering stopped and two of the little skunklets took aim in my general direction. But my youthful friend put me at ease.

"Don't you worry, Mr. Rood. Them squirt guns is only blanks."

In about four weeks, however, "them squirt guns" would begin to function. This would be a week or so after their eyes were open. In still another couple of weeks the babies would be out with the mother.

I've seen several troops of them in June and July, usually at night but sometimes in broad daylight. They poke along so closely behind the female that at first the whole retinue looks like a huge striped snake. You can follow distant progress in a meadow by the slowly waving grass.

They're kittens in actions as well as appearance. They play and tumble. At first they're pretty wobbly on their feet, and can get nearly as far by rolling as they can by walking. Later on, when they're out for a stroll, they often are literally nose-to-tail, following Mother's every move with comic seriousness. Each clump of grass and each mouse nest gets investigated four or five times. Sometimes when she stops suddenly, the whole line bumps together like cars in a freight train. And I have no doubt that an enemy would receive a salvo from not one but half a dozen tail-guns at once.

The family stays together most of the summer. They prefer insects and are great mousers, but they'll eat anything else they find. Turtle eggs are a special delicacy— which has undoubted value in regions where snapping turtles are claimed to be a menace to wild ducklings. Skunks are fond of yellowjacket grubs, too. They dig up the nests of the peppery hornets when they get a chance. This leaves things in a fine state for the next innocent passer-by.

"In fact," a game warden summed up the food habits of the skunk, "about the only thing a skunk asks when he sees something edible is 'Can I swallow it?' "

With a digestion like a cement mixer, the skunklets put on a good layer of fat by autumn. Now the family begins to break up. With the coming of chilly weather the skunks seek a place for a long winter nap. Sometimes they dig their own dens, but more often they appropriate another animal's burrow. This is often a woodchuck hole—with or without the woodchuck.

Finding a suitable place, a skunk investigates it for dormitory possibilities. Then he begins to cart in great masses of grass, leaves or ferns.

Often the woodchuck is already asleep in his own chamber. However, if he's still awake, he makes a show of sticking up for his rights. But the skunk merely continues his nest-building with all the aplomb of an engineer laying out a superhighway across a lawn. It's usually not long before two or three more skunks discover the hole, too. The woodchuck chatters his teeth, but the skunks stamp their feet—a warning that's unmistakable.

Finally the woodchuck gets the point. Then he has two choices—neither of which is to stand and fight, which would be distinctly non-habit-forming. He can either pack up and leave, or he can seal himself behind a wall of earth and leave the rest of the house to the hoboes.

A friend who runs a bulldozer once called me to view a winter 'chuck nest he had unearthed. It contained a sleepy woodchuck, five drowsy skunks and a frightened rabbit, for good measure. "I've known 'em to have as many as ten skunks in a den," he assured me.

While the 'chuck goes into a deep hibernation, the skunk seems to suffer from insomnia. We've seen him on balmy winter nights looking for food, like a man in pajamas raiding the icebox. During such times, the pinch of hunger in his stomach may force him to the farmer's barn or garbage pail. If he arrives at the barn, happy the farmer should be, for he'll clean out the mice and rats. However, if the "barn" happens to be a chickenhouse, the meal of rodents may be varied with eggs or even roosting birds.

Occasionally mother skunk remembers such forays later when her babies are born. Then she brings them back for an encore. At such times one or more of the babies may be captured.

The black-eyed little creatures make engaging pets—the younger they're captured the better. "But it's a mistake to remove their scent glands," my game warden friend informed me. "Skunks are reluctant to use their weapons, anyway. I've had several for pets and have never yet had one make a mistake. And what defense does a deodorized skunk have against even a determined tomcat? His legs are too short and his movements are too slow to defend himself. You've removed his one means of protection."

As I write these words, the spring evening is fast creeping over the Vermont hillside. As on several occasions previously, the breeze brings me the scent of the unhurried little pacifist who's seen from the Atlantic to the Pacific, from Canada into Mexico. The Algonquins called him "seganku," from which we get his common name today. He's also known as stinkweasel (he is actually a member of the weasel family) and polecat—although the true polecat is a ferretlike animal of the Old World.

But the name I like best is one which fits the odor that comes in my window on the breeze. It's the tongue-in-cheek scientific name by which biologists know him.

The name? *Mephitis mephitis.*

Its meaning? Roughly translated, it means "poison gas." And to borrow a phrase, thereby hangs a tale.

Fur-coated
Landscaper

RONALD ROOD:
On the Beaver

ROBERT CANDY Illustrations

YOU CAN NEVER TELL ABOUT BEA-vers. When the first few sticks appeared in a line across the New Haven River in front of our property, we were perplexed.

"Beavers, Dad? Do you think beavers are actually trying to dam up the *river?*"

It didn't make sense. The ends of the sticks, chiseled to a point by those four strong rodent teeth, plainly showed the work of beavers. And most of them were jammed in the sand butt first, so their branches would catch leaves and floating débris.

But our New Haven River was too swift for any beaver pond. It had turned the machinery in a dozen mills, whirled the dynamos for a power plant, and had once gone on a rampage through Lincoln and torn the town in half. Though it appeared mild enough now in the dry season, the first fall flood would wipe out any dam they could ever build.

Where was the fabled engineering genius of the beaver, if they were going to try to tame such a stream?

The dam grew night after night. Heavy branches, cut from the aspens and alders near by, formed the framework. These were loaded with pats of mud, sod and pebbles until they became watertight. A large rock six feet out in the river served as a bulwark.

Finished, the dam lay quietly at the lower end of its pool, while the water whispered over the entire forty feet of its edge.

The rains finally came in November. It drizzled for several days. The river foamed over its banks. We sloshed down the road to see what was left of the beaver dam. Sure enough, it was gone.

"Now, how are they going to build it back?" the children wanted to know. "There'll probably be high water in the river until spring."

And there, of course, was the answer. At last the beavers had the deep water they needed. And, by living in the bank of the river instead of the conventional hut of sticks and mud, they would survive through the winter. They had just built a one-shot dam—merely for a summer home.

Our furry neighbors followed this same routine for three years. Pioneers in this stretch of river, they have, like many another pioneer, learned to "make do" under the conditions at hand. If industry is the first characteristic of the beaver, versatility is the second.

A beaver often tunnels through a riverbank to get somewhere, instead of making a laborious trip overland. Other times it creates waterways where none existed before. A beaver pond near us has been in use for years. The choice aspens, willows and alders have long since been cut, and the beavers have to search far afield for their twigs and tender bark. But a beaver out of water is clumsy and helpless, for all its twenty to fifty pounds or more. So they have carried their water with them.

To do this, they built a series of locks in a tiny stream which ran down to the pond. Every few feet they made a little dam of sod, brush and mud. These terraces served in two ways—as swim-lanes for the beavers to and from woodlands, and as waterways for floating branches and logs with little

effort. As they forage farther away from the main pond, they just build another lock in their hillside canal.

At the moment, the system has more than half a dozen locks, each with side branches. They total several hundred feet. No other wild animal on earth, I'm told, purposely so changes the landscape to suit its ends. Dams have been recorded nearly half a mile long and fourteen feet high.

A resourceful beaver pulled an old trick on a friend of mine. "My dog cornered it in some rushes next to shore," he told me. "It was limping badly by the time I arrived. I called off the dog, and you never saw such a change in a beaver. Its limp disappeared, just like that, and it made a rush for the water.

"Then I caught on. Sure enough, a few feet away I saw some little webbed footprints and a patch of muddy water. Old mamma beaver had just been keeping Tippy busy 'til all the kids were safe."

In reality, "old mamma" has a lethal set of buck teeth. Orange, slightly curved, two and a half inches long including roots, they can slice through a four-inch tree in twenty minutes. The Indians used them for chisels to shape wood and bone. But the beaver would rather seek flight than fight. It swims slowly through the pond, paddling with its large webbed hind feet, steering with its flat scaly tail. Its squared-off nose, nearsighted eyes and round little ears sample the surroundings.

No matter how quietly we steal up, it remains suspicious. Alarmed, it dives, whacking its tail with a *ker-plunk* like a heavy stone dropped in the water. Sometimes it stays under for ten minutes. In the winter, it can remain even longer, breathing air that has been trapped beneath the ice.

All summer and fall we can watch our beaver neighbors at work. We often take a flashlight to help us, for they don't seem to mind the glare. One after the other, they bring green branches and disappear beneath the surface. Two winters ago I discovered for myself what they did with them. Through the ice I could see dozens of branches in a well-packed pile. So plentiful is the underwater pantry that beavers actually gain weight in winter.

Once, while I was kneeling on the ice and peering down, a great sleek body swept past—one of my friends on his way to the winter storehouse. The dense fur, trapping a coat of air as insulation against the freezing water, seemed cloaked in silver. It almost hid the dark brownish-black which is the normal color.

A good-sized beaver lodge may be fifteen feet or more in diameter. Made of sticks, mud and turf, it looks like a strange mounded island in the pond, or built out from shore. Inside is a hollow room, high enough in record specimens to accommodate a standing man. An abandoned one I looked into was three and a half feet high, with a raised floor of dry wood chips.

It's here, in the spring after a midwinter mating, that up to five kits are born. Helpless at first, they depend on their wet-furred mother as she comes through the underwater entrance to the lodge to nurse them. They yip and whine like puppies, although I've never heard a beaver give voice outside the lodge. By summer they are out snipping vegetation with their mother, chasing each other, and spatting the water with their flat little tails, whether there's danger around or not.

The male leaves the family chores to his mate. He finds a den of his own for a while. But he may be back with her while the kits are still growing. The entire family often winters over in a single lodge, sometimes with last year's grown children as well. The older children leave for good in the spring. They set out to establish families of their own. This wanderlust is what keeps the beavers spreading.

A winter family may produce enough heat in the lodge to send up a thin wisp of steam, which rises through a flue to the outside air like smoke from a tepee. In fact, the Indians, looking at the lives of their beaver neighbors, concluded that they were really people who had been changed into animals. The beavers' little handlike front feet heightened this illusion, as did their habit of tucking the ten-inch tail under their bodies as a cushion when they sat.

One autumn day I came across a beaver post office. This was a spot along a bank with a dozen little mud patties on it. Each passing beaver had carefully fashioned a patty, gravely deposited a bit of musky castoreum on it from glands near the tail, and added it to the pile. Thus he affixed his name to the roll and duly announced his presence to other beavers. It's this castoreum, used sometimes as a fixative in perfumes, which gives the beaver its scientific name, *Castor canadensis,* the Canadian perfumer.

About as common in Vermont as anywhere, the beaver is also known throughout almost all of North America. Pursuit of the lustrous fur sped the settlement of Canada enormously and opened a great part of our own West. The Astor fortune was built on beaver pelts, and they were long a medium of exchange over thousands of square miles. A friend of mine has a Hudson's Bay blanket in his trunk, marked with four stripes: value, four beaver skins.

Castor plays an even more important role which we're just beginning to appreciate. Six years ago a pair of beavers moved into a wooded valley a few miles from my home. You could step across its single little stream. Today there's a two-acre pond there. It contains a good supply of fish. A pair of colorful wood ducks have nested

there for two summers, along with other water birds. The water table has been raised, and the fire danger to the whole valley has plummeted. Last fall I noticed a little summer cabin along the shore.

This story is being repeated all over Vermont, for the little forester is on the upswing. Fur values are just moderate (fifteen to twenty dollars for a good pelt), so there's less trapping than in the days when a thirty-inch beaver sold for a dollar an inch. Cut-over woodlands, long solid with large trees, are coming up to beaver-sized aspen and other favorite foods. Abandoned farmland supplies less than its share of troublesome dogs and inquisitive farm boys. Although a waddling baby beaver is easy prey on land for a host of predators, the adults have little to fear except for an occasional otter. Hence the beavers who reach maturity find that the odds are in their favor.

But there's another side, too. Eager beavers sometimes get out of hand. A friend of mine watched his meadow hayfield dis-

appear under a foot of water. It backed clear up under his fence and onto his neighbor's land.

When he finally dynamited the dam, he also blasted his neighbor's friendship. The neighbor, it turned out, had quietly released a load of trout into the pond. Now he saw his money go, literally and figuratively, down the drain.

My neighbor downriver lost her choice French lilac to a beaver gourmet. And many a road commissioner will reach white heat about how a country road was flooded in spite of his best efforts. For a colony of beavers can easily outstrip a man with a shovel.

The problem is that a given piece of land can support just so many animals of *any* species. They're all part of a complicated natural balance. If man goes ahead and kills off their enemies, or tinkers with the balance in some other way, they may increase faster than the land can hold them. Then, like some of our Vermont beavers,

they overrun the place. You might say the land could become super-saturated with beavers—in more ways than one.

In some states, such as Massachusetts, beavers have been live-trapped and moved to areas where they can frolic all they wish. In the West they are even flown to inaccessible spots and dropped in self-opening cages. But here in Vermont such action has little effect, according to the Fish and Game Department. Most of the spots have already been picked over by the beavers themselves. If it's not good beaver country, they move.

Starting sometime around 1950 they moved from the saturated area around Groton and gradually spread out, somewhat as an ice-cube tray will fill to the farthest corners as water is poured into one section. In 1961 more than thirty-five hundred of them were taken over all of Vermont's fourteen counties during the late winter trapping season—nearly three times as many as were taken ten years before.

An acquaintance of mine is an officer of

a youth camp. The staff was delighted when a pair of beavers moved in at the lower end of the little lake. "The campers used to watch them at dusk," he said. "One evening we saw one nibbling at something on the ground. Nobody bothered to figure what it was until we tried to get water the next morning. He had gnawed right through the three-inch plastic pipe that went out into the lake.

"This was just the start of our troubles. A week later our prize weeping willow lay on the ground. It was cut into stove-length pieces. Several canoe paddles disappeared. The beavers were starting on the pilings of the dock when we finally got them live-trapped.

"Another camp heard about our visitors and asked us if they could have them. So we wet them down good to keep their foot-pads from cracking and shipped 'em out. So far, we're still good friends with the folks in the other camp, but I haven't dared to ask about their beavers."

An old-timer told a group of us about a beaver family that caused a lot of trouble where a crew was trying to lay out a road. Each night the beavers would build up the dam and flood the area; each day the crew would tear it down.

"It got to be pretty tiresome to the crew," he said. "And I guess the beavers got tired, too. One morning the men couldn't believe their eyes. The dam was in place once again, but there was no water behind it.

"The crew went to look things over. They found that the beavers had put a piece of stovepipe right through the dam with a shut-off damper in it. They'd used the water all night and then opened the valve in the morning to let it out."

He stared at us, daring anyone to question such a whopper. But nobody even cracked a smile.

After all, you can never tell about beavers.

101

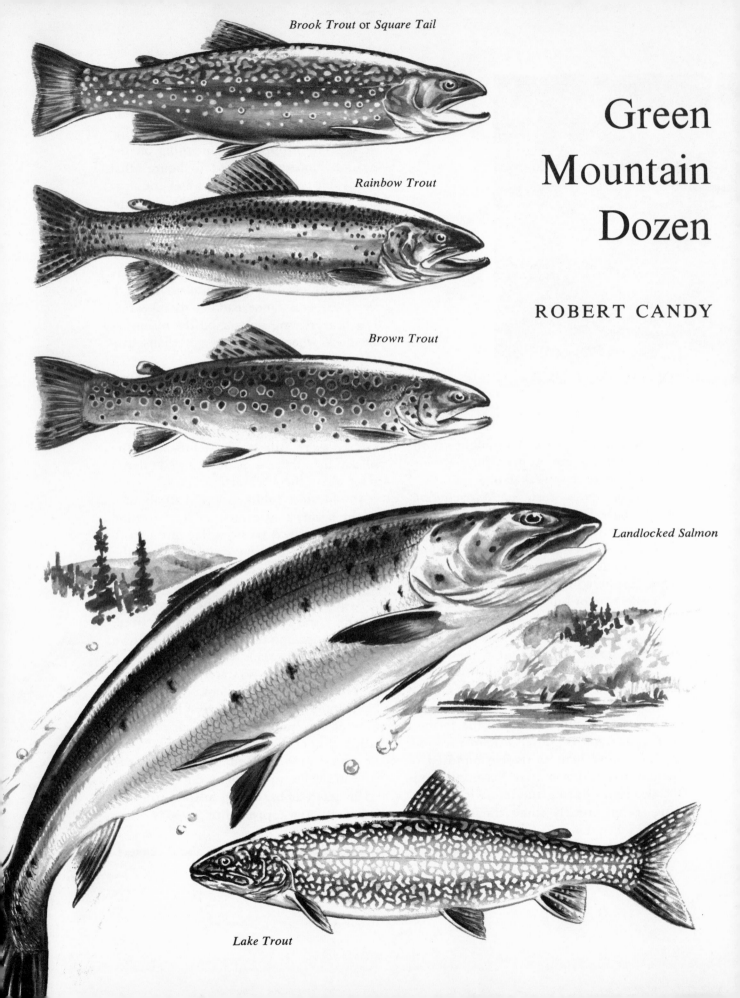

Brook Trout or Square Tail

Rainbow Trout

Brown Trout

Green Mountain Dozen

ROBERT CANDY

Landlocked Salmon

Lake Trout

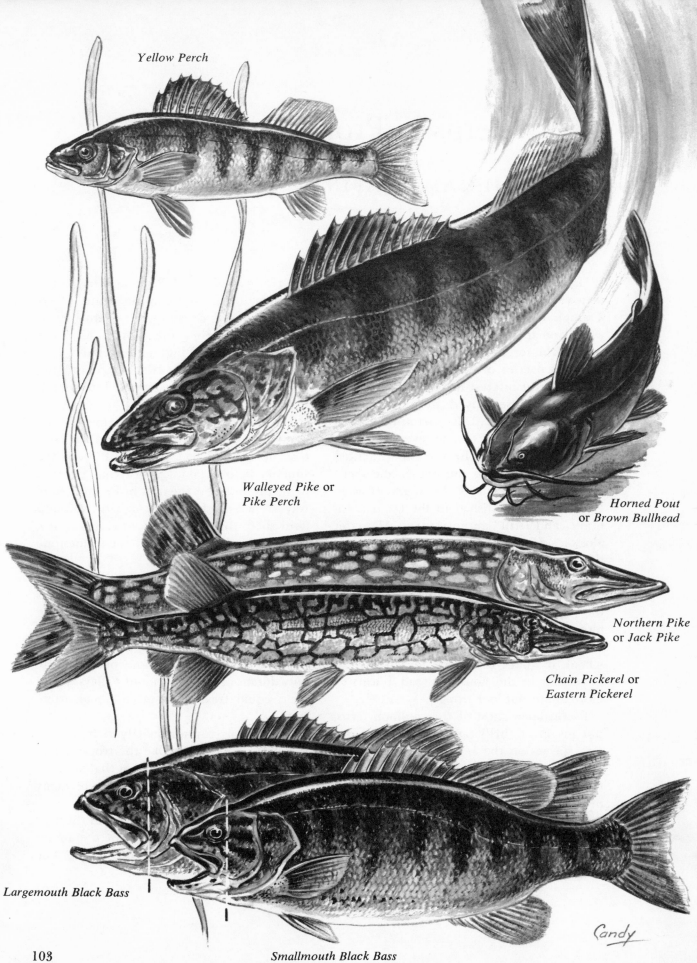

Yellow Perch

Walleyed Pike or
Pike Perch

Horned Pout
or Brown Bullhead

Northern Pike
or Jack Pike

Chain Pickerel or
Eastern Pickerel

Largemouth Black Bass

Candy

103

Smallmouth Black Bass

Ferns in Profusion

MIRIAM CHAPIN

WHEN I WAS A GIRL IN PITTSFORD, that village was a center of fern study. Though I didn't realize it, several people who lived there were known to the scientific world for their work with ferns and their discoveries of certain hybrids which were of great interest to botanists.

Grace Woolson lived in a low white house at Pittsford Mills, surrounded by a garden where she tended every possible variety of ferns, and she also experimented with raising them in the house. She spent much time on her book, *Ferns and How to Grow Them,* published in the Garden Library and still authoritative. Margaret Slosson's *How Ferns Grow,* a more scientific treatise, was another product of that time.

It was Dr. Swift, the family doctor of all the region, who first roused my interest in ferns. He suggested to my father that, since I was a sickly child and seldom went to school, it would be a good idea if instead of staying in the house to read I learned more about outdoor things.

I soon knew most of the common ferns, but my great thrill came when I found a rare species on the Limestone Rock. This was a great slab of different texture from the surrounding ledges, which reared up nearly twenty feet in the air beside a hollow in my grandfather's sheep pasture. I picked a frond, brought it home, and searched through the books. I decided it

was really *Asplenium Ruta-muraria,* noted as "uncommon, found on limestone." Next time the doctor drove up the avenue lined with maples below our house, his little Morgan horse pulling the covered buggy at a good pace and his Irish setters ranging ahead, I ran out and stopped him to tell him of my find.

He agreed that I was right, and praised me for recognizing it, but I found out later that he himself had planted it there the summer before, taking a bit from a clump he had found near the falls in Proctor. Anyway, he was glad to know it had lived and flourished. It was still flourishing a few years ago, when I climbed the Limestone Rock once again.

So it is no accident that botanical books note "Pittsford, Vt." or "Proctor, Vt." as the locale for many unusual ferns, along with "Willoughby Lake" and "Mt. Mansfield." It means that eager collectors have combed the terrain at those places. Probably dozens of other Vermont valleys would yield equal treasure if given equal attention.

Vermont is extraordinarily rich in fern varieties. None is big like the tropical tree ferns, which are like the ones that went to make coal eons ago, but they are of many kinds.

The fronds we see, what we call "ferns," with the brown spore cases on the under side, are only half their life cycle. The

Interrupted fern

other half is a tiny green speck, which grows from one of the spores when it drops on damp ground. This green dot sinks rootlets into the soil, and bears on its upper surface microscopic male and female organs, not complex enough to be called stamens and pistils as in flowers. This is one of nature's early devices for securing fertilization of a cell, not yet complex enough to be called a seed. When several plants grow near together, there may be cross-fertilization, and even the crossing of species to make new varieties.

Ferns grow from their rootstocks too, pushing on year after year by means of these tough underground stems, sending up new clumps every few inches. As anyone who has tried to transplant them knows, these rootstocks may extend a long way from the original plant. And with this continued growth the fern is practically immortal, in favorable conditions.

105

Ferns are closely related to the horsetails, those gritty tufts that spring up in the mud beside every country lane, and to the trailing pine which carpets our Vermont woods. All of them are experiments in evolution, earlier than pines and spruces.

Of our true ferns, we in Vermont have three families. The commonest example of the Adder's Tongues—nothing to do with the little yellow lily with the spotted leaves that is everywhere in maple woods in spring—is the Rattlesnake Fern, found in the same sort of sugarbush, but in August.

You may think it is a flowering plant gone to seed, for its spore case is on a stem raised from the center of a deeply cut frond. But it isn't, and it has some rare cousins you will be lucky to find if you start collecting, like moonwort and the little grape ferns. It is easy to see why they were named, for their spore cases do look like tiny bunches of green grapes, but why the rattlesnake fern? Did some settler or some Indian medicine man think it would cure snakebite?

All sorts of curative and magic properties used to be attributed to ferns, but except for male fern (Aspidium) which does have some utility as a home remedy for tapeworm, most of them must be valued for their beauty and greenness alone. Fern seed, supposed to confer the gift of invisibility, undoubtedly would if it existed. It was to be gathered from the bracken on the Eve of St. John, but alas, no one ever proved its sorcerer's power.

The Flowering Fern family is made up of our three most conspicuous and handsome ferns, the Regal, the Interrupted, and the Cinnamon. I have sort of a suspicion that most people are really sure of only two kinds of ferns, Maidenhair, which they are all too apt to exclaim over and then dig up, and Brakes, under which name they lump all big ferns, the three just mentioned and

the real bracken. Yet they are very different, and easy to tell apart.

The Cinnamon Fern is a big cluster of rather coarse fronds, with its cinnamon-colored spore cases borne high in the center of the cluster. The Interrupted Fern is the one of which you say "it must have something the matter with it—why, all the leaves in the middle of the stalk are blighted." For the spore cases come half way up the stalk, and they do look as if a few leaves had caught some disease. Once you notice that they are all alike, you will look more closely and see that this is just an odd trick of growth. The Regal Fern is quite the loveliest of all these large ferns. It grows on the edge of swampy land, and its finely cut leaves, with its great clumps often four feet high, make a striking sight.

All these ferns can be transplanted, and make wonderful background for iris in the garden. All ferns want acid wood soil, and most of them want shade.

Nine-tenths of our Vermont ferns belong to the Polypody family. Polypody is the small evergreen fern that makes a cover of green over rocks in wet woods. You can strip a whole sheet of it off a slab, roots, moss and tangled fronds. Each plant looks like a small Christmas Fern. It is sturdy, it adds greatly to the beauty of the rocks, and it is of scientific interest because it has a lot of variations in the shape of fronds, no one knows why.

Much more work can be done on this question of variations and cross-breeding, and ferns are one of the valuable subjects. It all leads up to the big controversy on how hereditary factors are transmitted, and whether acquired characteristics can be passed on, as the Russian Lysenko believes they can. The wide range of shapes in Polypody might some day give a clue. This one species gives its name to the whole family, which includes our woods ferns.

Among them is Maidenhair, the lovely spreading fern with the wiry black stem, so hard to transplant, and so short-lived when picked that one begs the passer-by not to disturb it. Yet it is so tempting that it has become scarce, in spite of efforts to preserve it.

The many kinds of Shield Ferns come in here; you will be well advanced in fern lore before you learn to name them all. Then there are the little dainty Spleenworts, not really rare, but unnoticed until you learn how to look for them. Of these the Ebony is one of the most ornamental and the commonest, with its stiff black shiny stems. Several rare kinds grow in Vermont, besides my find on the Limestone Rock.

The Walking Leaf is one of the oddest of all plants of any kind. It doesn't look like other ferns, and it doesn't behave like them. It has a frond shaped like a long narrow arrowhead, with a fine thread of a runner from the tip. Like a strawberry runner, it feels around for a bit of soil, turns downward into the earth, and in a little while produces a new plant there. Soon the Walking Leaf covers a rock with a green mat, leaves twisted and woven one over the other. Yet in spite of this ingenuity, and the fact that it has spores like other ferns, it is not very common. It will grow in the house, if the right rock and soil is provided, and its "walking" is a curious performance to watch.

Then you may have noticed that some ferns have little almost transparent bulblets on the under side of their fronds, as well as spore cases. They are the Bladder Ferns, and the tiny bulblets will also form new plants if they fall in suitable places.

The Hay-scented Fern is common in dry upland pastures; most people know the fragrance that rises from it as their boots crush it. The Sensitive Fern (Onoclea) is the rather coarse-leaved one in beds in damp sunny places. The Oak and Beech ferns are fairly easy to find in dry woods.

The Christmas Fern—the one florists use all year—is evergreen, and is to be found flattened but still green on hillsides when the snow goes away. In bygone years many Vermonters took to their mountains every October to gather this fern for shipment to Boston.

Brakes, the true bracken, are common everywhere, and in many countries. The big, coarse, spreading fronds grow by roadsides or on any wasteland. Their little fuzzy unrolling fiddleheads, along with those of the Cinnamon and Interrupted ferns, are the greens that country people cook in spring. They're good, too, with an odd woodsy flavor.

There are several books to start you on your study of ferns. Your local library almost surely has one or more. All keys to species are based on the spore cases, though you will quickly learn to tell the common kinds by a glance at the frond. In the Polypody family, some have the cases in dots, some in chains, some like Maidenhair with the edge of the leaf rolled over to cover them. Once you become an enthusiast, you will hardly rest content until you have found and identified a species new to your locality, or perhaps even discovered some brand new variety.

Then they'll name it for you, and you will be assured of a minor immortality.

Gulls

of
The Four Brothers

EDWIN WAY TEALE

BULLATY-LOMEO Photographs

WHEN WE THINK OF VERMONT birds, we think of bobolinks over lush meadows of spring or of the chorus of thrushes at twilight on wooded Mt. Mansfield. We think of songbirds, of land birds. For the state of Vermont consists almost entirely of land. Of its nearly ten thousand square miles, only three hundred and forty are composed of water.

Yet any time from early May far into June, if you approach the small cluster of The Four Brothers islands, only about three and a half miles off Shelburne Point in central Lake Champlain, you'll find yourself in the midst of a scene reminiscent of the ocean shore. The air is filled with gulls. In a white cloud, thousands of screaming birds mill about your boat. They comprise a nesting colony of ring-bills that has been increasing year by year for more than a decade.

Three and a half centuries ago, on the spring day when Samuel de Champlain dis-

108

covered the lake that bears his name, he was accompanying a party of Hurons and Algonquins, then at war with the Iroquois. A naturalist as well as an explorer, Champlain noted the wildlife he encountered. The fact that he was impressed by the number of gulls he saw at the time is reflected in the name he bestowed on one of the principal rivers flowing through northern Vermont and emptying into Lake Champlain. He called it *La Mouette,* the French for gull, a name that in succeeding years became corrupted into Lamoille. Today, a county as well as a river bears this name.

Two centuries after Champlain, it was John James Audubon's opinion that the ring-bill was the most abundant gull in North America. In appearance, it suggests a smaller herring gull—the bird usually referred to as "the seagull"—but the dark band that completely encircles the yellow bill of the adult distinguishes it from the larger bird. Its flight is more buoyant and airy than that of the heavier herring gull. The ring-bill, also, is more likely to be found inland, on lakes and along the larger streams.

During the days of the atrocious plume trade in the latter years of the nineteenth century, when millions of feathered creatures were slaughtered to provide milliners with decorations for hats, the wings of these gulls were in special demand. By the time they were finally protected by the Migratory Bird Treaty Act of 1918, their numbers had been vastly reduced. It has been only in comparatively recent years that their dramatic comeback has been achieved. Now it is estimated that eighty or ninety percent of the gulls on Lake Champlain are ring-bills. At some season of the year, these birds are found virtually from coast to coast as well as along both the Atlantic and Pacific shores.

Of the Brothers, it is the largest and most central one that the gulls have chosen for their nesting area. The colony occupies the northeastern half of this eight-acre island. Here the land is higher, grassy and more free of trees and bordered on the east by a cliff. The nests are densely concentrated but a few feet apart, each pair guarding against intrusion of its territory by either adults or young. Almost always the ring-billed gulls establish their nesting colonies on islands. There the eggs and young, two or three in each nest, are safe from foxes, skunks, weasels and other land predators. Also on islands civilization is less likely to encroach on the birds. Ring-bills, far more quickly than herring gulls, desert their nesting areas when they are disturbed.

James D. Stewart, biologist of the Vermont Fish and Game Department, has kept the Four Brothers gulls under observation for a number of years. He has seen their numbers grow from a few hundred, in 1949, to "a conservative four thousand" in 1964. Each year a few herring gulls raise their young around the perimeter of the ring-bills' nesting area. Their eggs are laid two or three weeks earlier than those of the ring-bills. A flourishing colony of black-crowned night herons occupies the treetops of a smaller, more wooded neighboring island.

It is during their nesting period that the gulls, like other birds, are most active in gathering food. Parents of some species travel staggering distances day after day while feeding their young. In the course of a single day a chimney swift may fly as much as one hundred miles gathering insects from the air for its brood. The white pelicans nesting on islands in the Great Salt Lake in Utah make hundred-mile round trips to fish in fresh water in order to supply food for their hungry young. Over Lake Champlain the gulls are on the wing

all day long and far into the evening, alert for the minnows and small smelt they carry back to their nestlings.

The diet of the ring-bill is infinitely more varied than that of the herring gull. Both are scavengers as well as hunters of living food. But the smaller ring-bills wander inland over fields and meadows, sometimes hawking about like swallows to snap flying grasshoppers and beetles from the air, at other times following plows to obtain the insects and earthworms that are brought to the surface. Through their destruction of agricultural pests, these birds are of considerable economic importance.

They often follow ships miles from land to feed on refuse thrown overboard. Along the shore, they occasionally run about in the manner of sandpipers, picking up small crustaceans from the wet beach. Ofttimes they assemble in screaming flocks at town dumps, and in the West they have been observed feeding along highways on ground squirrels killed by automobiles. This versatility in securing food is considered a mark of the ring-bills' intelligence.

After the nesting season is over the members of the Lake Champlain colony break up into small flocks, leading a more leisurely life, using rocky points and shoals as resting places. At such times the white birds are often seen ten or a dozen miles inland. Some wander forty or fifty miles from the water of the lake. They may sometimes be encountered flying over fields in the very shadow of Mt. Mansfield and the chain of the Green Mountains. During the summer many move northward along the St. Lawrence River in Canada. But with the coming of winter the birds turn south, frequently following the waterway of the lower Hudson River to the coast.

Thousands of nestlings have been banded at the Lake Champlain colony. These bands have helped trace the winter movement of the gulls. Some have been found as far away as Florida and even the Gulf Coast of Texas. But when the ice breaks up at the end of winter the gulls come drifting back. In the warm days of May, The Four Brothers once more take on the animation, the sound and movement, the special interest that is imparted by their city of nesting gulls.

112

Treasures of the Wetlands

CAUGHT IN THE GLACIER-FORMED pockets of Vermont's on-end typography are numerous bogs that date from the end of the last ice age, about twelve thousand years ago. Swampy also, but very different in origin, are the broader marshes, found sometimes in wide river valleys and especially along Lake Champlain's southeastern shores. The following descriptions of the secret worlds of the wetlands are by Charles Cleveland Johnson and Philip F. Allan.

The bogs began as deep ponds, which, over the ages, have filled with decaying organic matter that becomes peat. A rough rule of thumb, not allowing for wide variations in climate conditions, held that a bog accumulated around one foot of peat every five hundred years. Since several Vermont bogs are thirty feet of quaking peat deep, this rule could date them back to perhaps 10,000 B.C.

All through bogs from top to bottom are pollen grains that have been deposited down the centuries. Experts in pollen studies can reconstruct the whole amazing sequence of plants that have grown in Vermont since the glaciers melted away—from the dwarf willows of the first tundra to the species in our present-day woodlands.

The bogs are of two types. Acid bogs are characterized by sphagnum moss, blueberries, Labrador tea, black spruce—and especially by the insect-eating plants. Flora of the alkaline bogs includes white cedar, white spruce, tamaracks, sedges, and the rare orchids.

Marshes, usually not so old or so deep as bogs, are formed by alluvial deposits that have been washed down from nearby, overflowing streams and lakes. Although they hold fewer mysteries, they too often contain interesting flora and fauna which, if not so rare, are more profuse, and follow definite and interlocking seasonal cycles. Comparatively shallow and with firm bottoms, the marshland is usually safer to explore, and is too wet to support many trees.

W. R. H., Jr.

Staying Unspoiled

"Unspoiled Vermont" is the guiding slogan—in a quite unpromotional sense—for the state chapter of the National Nature Conservancy. Its members recognize the need for new highways, power lines, suburbias, and factories, yet they are determined to save unusual wild habitats and places of rare beauty from casual obliteration.

Information about their efforts in Vermont may be obtained from James W. Marvin, 303 Swift Street, South Burlington 05401, or Perry H. Merrill, 200 Elm Street, Montpelier 05602. The address of the National Nature Conservancy is 1522 K Street N.W., Washington, D. C. 20005.

The Bogs

CHARLES CLEVELAND JOHNSON Story and Photographs

ROBERT CANDY Illustrations

SCATTERED WIDELY THROUGH Vermont are remnants of glacier-made pools that are among the state's most interesting natural phenomena. Seldom large in size—none like our great swamps of the South—they are of natural interest far out of proportion to their physical area.

These bogs that lie in pockets between hills and mountains are typified by a tiny pond in the rough center of an open area which is irregularly girded by a mixed stand of swamp trees. Black spruce, balsam, tamarack, white cedar, birches of several species, and swamp maple are the usual forest growth. The black spruce ventures closest to the open water. The thousands of years that have elapsed since the last glacier melted northward, permitted vegetation such as sphagnum moss and other water-loving plants to grow inward from the pool's original edges—creating new land from their organic remains, which, at last, is firm enough to support the trees whose roots draw sustenance from the peat and marl base.

Walk over the damp spongy ground at a bog's edge—toward its center—out onto the sphagnum. Suddenly the earth quakes under your feet. Each step causes vibrations in the moss cover for yards around, and you realize that this is no longer terra firma but only a plant mass that supports your weight above land in the slow process of formation. Not far beneath your feet is decomposed vegetation with the consistency of hasty pudding.

But why venture into such treacherous places? Why not be satisfied to view such locations from their extreme edges? One of the answers to these questions is that a bog is often a place of rare beauty—an absolutely unspoiled natural setting—a place where one seems suddenly remote from all civilization and walking out of time itself. Something of this Thoreau must have had in mind when he wrote, "I enter a swamp as a sacred place."

Here spring and summer bring wildflowers in profusion and exciting color variety. The woods that bound most of these bogs are particularly rich in spring flora, the forest glades often nearly carpeted with violets—yellow, blue and white.

And in such places I've found bunchberry in mats so dense as to require a detour lest a straight course despoil them. In thicker wooded areas the painted trillium, heartleaf-lily, and gold thread are among the flowers to greet you. These are but suggestions, for here you'll find most of the flowers of spring of those species requiring moist earth for their happiest growth; while scattered about in the not too dense areas, flowering shrubs and trees like the swamp maple lend their high-level color accent to the scene.

114

In the central open area bordering the pool, cotton grass, laurel, Labrador tea, and cranberry are among those flowers that add their note of visual beauty to the harmony of yellow, red, brown, blue and green that is the sphagnum, sedges, trees, water and sky. Nor should we omit the water-lilies—frequent residents of the pool itself.

One familiar with such environs may well well recall a day in May when sights and sounds of Nature included mass and variety of the common wildflowers at their loveliest, leaf buds bursting on the hardwoods, the scurry of small game surprised by a quiet approach, and the height of the warbler migration—thrilling both eye and ear. Such a combination is for one's memory bank, a fund to be drawn on when some other pleasant experience recalls this one.

But as many *do* know, there is treasure in our bogs far exceeding this already banked. Thoreau explored little of Vermont. He should have done more—for these same bogs are the favorite haunts of our most beautiful terrestrial orchids, some species of which may be found throughout most of our late spring and summer.

It may surprise some folks familiar with the orchids of our florist shops to learn that Vermont is especially rich in this flower family. Of America's approximately two hundred native species and varieties, at least fifty are residents of this state. And of these Vermont residents no less than two-thirds have chosen the bogs either as their only dwelling place or as one type of location where they flourish. As to one's chances of finding several species growing in a single environment, it's worth noting, I think, that thirty-three species have been found in one five-square-mile Vermont area.

Generally speaking our native orchids are smaller than the featured horticultural species, but those who know the rare beauty of the ladyslipper clan, and Arethusa, Calypso, Calopogon, and our several species of fringed orchids (purple, orange, and white) regard their smaller perfection as rivaling or surpassing the florist's exotics. All of these are natives of Vermont's bogs —each species waiting to greet you in one or many locations from May until midsum-

115

Orange Fringed Orchid

Sundew

mer as its flowering turn arrives.

As long as I live, for me there will be something mysteriously intriguing about a bog. It may be that childhood training, which warned of breaking through and disappearing beneath what appeared to be fairly solid ground, could have instilled both fear and fascination. And let no one show disrespect for a sphagnum surface! When ground quakes under your feet you're well advised to move with caution. I've explored a lot of bogs. I've never fallen through. I don't want to. And if this article inspires some bog hunting for orchids, you be careful, too! In one bog photographed in 1961 we poked a pole easily down through seventeen feet of the stuff on which we stood and didn't touch bottom.

The reward for your search? Who has ever looked upon the beauty of Arethusa in her natural setting without a gasp at her perfection? Through the late spring and summer there are surprises each week that include such orchids as Calypso. You may well find, too, the exquisite Calopogon whose second Latin name means "little beauty," and five species of ladyslippers in

bloom for weeks from the first May appearance of rams-head, through the pink, and yellows, and finally the usually accepted queen of them all, Reginae, the showy ladyslipper.

Spring often brings the coralroot in the wooded wet areas at the open bog edges and the green and white spires of the rein orchids, hyperborea and dilatata. And to name only a few others, late June and July finds the Pogonia tribe in all its glory and the marvelous blooms of the large purple fringed orchid, about which Thoreau complained that it grew only where moose and moose-hunters could see it.

These are but a few of the orchids awaiting the explorer in the bogs of Vermont, and although those named include the more beautiful ones, there are others available for discovery into autumn and the last blooms of ladies-tresses.

But the explorer will find still other thrills in the bog's open area in the large colonies of carnivorous plants—peculiar in appearance and fascinating in their ways of life. For here are the pitcher plants, whose odd leaves and blossoms are both

116

strangely handsome, and the very different but no less intriguing sundew.

I once watched hundreds of freshly hatched dragonflies of a small species become trapped inexorably at a bog's edge by a colony of sundew and then to await digestion as supplemental diet to soil nutriment. And how many pitcher-plant leaves I've investigated to view the remains of insects who found the pitcher mouth a one-way street to oblivion!

Our forefathers, both American and European, and the American Indians as well, had high regard for many wildflowers, including orchids, as alleviants and cures for their ills. Of our more common wildflowers, many of which you'll find on any spring or summer venture to a Vermont bog, violets have been used as herbs; and wild ginger has been used as an antidote for snakebite and for sciatica, difficult respiration, and various other diseases. Indian cucumber root has been used as a medicine. The root of our common adders-tongue boiled in water was supposed to be good for the teeth. Although not a flower, the walking fern was made into a concoction for treating diseases of the kidneys and liver.

These are but samples of the herbalist folklore, which, projected into the orchid family, finds many species playing a prominent part in medicine.

Whatever may be thought of our ancestors' knowledge of plant use as materia medica, we may be a bit surprised at the number of our New England orchid species that had already been located by European botanists and transplanted to British botanical gardens prior to 1810. Our large purple fringed orchid reached England in 1777; Calypso in 1805; and Calopogon had reached Holland even earlier.

Our orchids are rare today—far more so than a hundred years ago—and in need of strict conservation. In addition to the woodsman's axe and the drains of encroaching civilization that have changed the character of many of our former orchid habitats, other factors have adversely affected their survival.

Promiscuous picking sadly depleted these species. And such picking had been preceded by bulb-snatchers who once found a market for their gleanings in herb doctors, who from them made salves and unguents and other cure-alls. Unfortunately when the herb doctors fell into disrepute, the bulb-snatchers found a new and better market in florists who featured native orchids for the home flower gardens.

Despite this sad note on man's destructiveness of some of the most beautiful things that God ever made, we still do have them in limited quantities in the bogs of Vermont. And if we will but use a little common sense and observe one simple rule we shall continue to have them. If you choose to visit these wonderlands, only your feet need leave their imprint. Be careful where you put them lest you crush a thing of beauty while observing that major but simple rule of the National Park Service—"Admire and leave for others to enjoy."

Ladyslipper

117

The Marshes

PHILIP F. ALLAN

ROBERT CANDY Illustrations

THE ROCK ON WHICH I SAT RE-membered the first warm sun of spring after the air had forgotten. Ten, and per-haps twenty millennia of warm suns and cool air, since the granite boulder was wrenched from a northward ledge by the last glacier, had sculptured my rock into a fairly comfortable seat. Infinitesimal expan-sions deep inside and equally small con-tractions outward, the results of alternate

118

heating and cooling, had rounded the an-
gular granite. The concave slabs exfoliated
from its surface now lay half-buried near
the base of the rock.

I drew my jacket a bit tighter. To the
west the sky was still roseate in the brief
twilight after sunset. Below me lay a small
marsh, about an acre in area. A chorus of
spring peepers welled up from the cold
waters at its center. At times, it seemed to

me that the individual voices were out of
cadence, then suddenly all of the hundreds
of singers were in rhythm. The sound recalled other marshes and other Hylidian
music-makers: the "tink-tank" orchestra in
a Maryland marsh where each frog seemed
to be clashing tiny copper cymbals; the
string ensemble of cricket frogs in Michigan; a glee club of the chorus frog in a
Texas marsh.

119

In one of the quiet intervals between songs I became aware of a faint rustling of leaves at the side of the rock. A spotted salamander hurried, in ungainly fashion, to a rendezvous in the marsh. Each leg seemed to operate on its own schedule in a tentative sort of way. But in spite of its apparent lack of co-ordination and its clumsiness the salamander must be accounted a success. For something like a hundred million years—roughly one hundred times as long as human beings have been around—salamanders have been making this annual pilgrimage to the Mecca of the marsh.

It is said that life came from the sea. But the emergence of salamanders, and indeed of all vertebrates including ourselves, no doubt took place in a fresh-water marsh. Most of our present-day amphibians have an aversion to salt water.

Now and then, among the spring peeper voices, I detected a "ker - r - r - ock." That is the spring song of the leopard frog. In a few more nights the rasping clucks of the black-masked wood frog would be added. Then the trills of the common American toad join the musical festival; and the pickerel frog with its low-pitched croak; and the banjo-string plinking of the green frog. The flat telephone ring of the gray tree frog is heard about a month after the peepers start, and last of all comes the familiar, warm-weather *jug-o-rum* of the bullfrog.

Thus, spring came to a small Vermont marsh. And with it came the fiddleheads of marsh and cinnamon ferns, the yellow-blooming cowslips, the "pur - ple E" song of the courting redwing, the first sunning of the painted turtle on a muskrat lodge, the garter snake slipping through the new green rushes at the water's edge, and the doe, heavy with twin fawns, seeking tender water-lily shoots.

Marshes are one of the more evanescent features of the landscape. We tend to think

of them as being there forever. But they come and go. Floods, silt deposits and the dead remains of plant life are the great makers of marsh. They also are the natural destroyers of marshlands, and in surprisingly few years—sometimes less than a century—a marsh may be converted to a meadow or a wooded swamp.

Man's activities have hastened some of these changes, for from the time of first settlement by our pioneer ancestors drainage has been practiced. Land tillage and lumbering have contributed to flooding and the deposition of sediment, thus obstructing some watercourses and creating marshes, or filling and putting an end to others. Many a present-day marsh in Vermont was once a hay meadow or crop field, now abandoned. And some such fields were once marshes.

Vermont is not as well endowed with natural marshes as are many states. There are, nevertheless, about fifty thousand acres, perhaps more, of them. The largest ones, and most extensive area of marsh, are found in the Champlain Valley. In general, the conditions that favor marsh development—highly erosive soils, slow meandering, silt-laden streams and gently undulating terrain or broad flat valleys—are not common in the state.

My little marsh, like the granite boulder, owed its existence to the glacier. The retreating ice left a relict pillar buried in the fine silt of an esker. With the warming climate, the top of the ice-pillar melted, giving birth to a pond. Even before the parent glacier disappeared up the valley, algae were growing in the icy pool and the tiny insects called springtails gathered in blue-gray blots at the water's edge. With the continued thawing, the water became deeper until, had someone tried to plumb its depths, it became one of the so-called "bottomless" ponds.

But other actions were taking place to reduce the pond's depth. Rainfall on the raw moraine carried soil into the depression. The first visiting black ducks brought seeds of Potamogeton and Najas, aquatic plants whose descendants are still there. Water-shield and water-lilies followed, and soon there were also floating mats of duckweed.

Willows and birches moved in behind the retreating glacier and after them came spruces, balsam and pine. Their pollen, carried by the south wind, floated on the pond surface for a time, then sank, waterlogged, to the bottom. The various layers of pollen can still be identified, and this serves scientists as one of the ways of dating glaciation.

As the pond waters warmed, brook trout invaded, and so did minnows and suckers. Spring thaws and summer thunderstorms brought leaves, twigs and silt into the pond. When maple, beech, ash and oak succeeded the conifers, there was, each autumn, a parti-colored shower of leaves on the water's surface. In the cool Vermont climate this rich organic deposit accumulated rapidly, accelerated by the water plantains, bur-reeds, arrowheads, pickerelweed, sedges, rushes and cattails that presently grew in the shallows.

Through the years the pond surface diminished in area and the water became ever shallower and warmer. Horned pout and grass pickerel largely replaced the trout. Today all that remains of the pond is an irregular shallow pool, fed and emptied by a little meandering brook and bordered by a marsh and wet meadow.

One summer afternoon I started for my favorite sitting rock. An old lightning-struck pine stands about twenty rods north of the marsh. At one time a pair of pileated woodpeckers excavated themselves a nest in it. I glanced toward the tree as I passed and thought I saw a small gray object fall from the hole. I started to investigate, when another popped out. So I stopped to watch. My binoculars revealed a tiny duckling at the foot of the tree. One after another, four more dropped the thirty feet from hole to the ground and, as I quietly watched, the mother wood duck led her brood to the marsh.

I had earlier seen a family of black ducks and found the multiple nests of a pair of long-billed marsh wrens in the cattails. Redwings had hatched and gone. But a pair of yellow warblers had a nest in the pussy willows on the west side, and yellowthroats nested in the tall bluejoint grass of the wet meadow. There, too, I had seen a

meadow jumping mouse, that odd little kangaroo that sleeps out the long Vermont winter snug underground.

In summer, the open water is a simmering soup of living creatures. Pollywogs of a half-dozen kinds wriggle in the shallow water. Whirligig beetles dance minuets on the surface. Pond skaters glide about, making, on the pond bottom, six black shadows of the depressed water film beneath their feet. Vampirish great red leeches undulate along, seeking a turtle or a human foot on which to make a meal. Minnows eat and are eaten by insects. Fierce dragonfly nymphs lurk about the plant roots under water, hoping to impale other immature insects, while their bright-hued parents hawk for mosquitoes overhead. I pulled a water-soaked stick from the pool and found on it several tiny hydras. Near by was a large jelly-ball of Bryozoa, or moss animals. A horsehair worm, which, as a child, I believed was actually a horsehair come to life, writhed in the water. Once it lived in the body of a cricket. Snails of

three species scrape up a meal on pondweed stalks and leaves.

Summer is flower time. There are white arrowheads and lavender pickerelweeds; pinks show in smartweed, grass pink and snakemouth. And, to me, a marsh would be incomplete without the dusty pink of joe-pye weed. Blues are well represented by the blue flag and lobelia. Sometimes you can find the purple fringed orchid or the yellowish-white ladies-tresses. Rattlesnake manna-grass, so named for its segmented inflorescence, grows well out into the water. So does the saw-edged rice cut-grass, whose ricelike seeds are a staple of the ducks.

Where the brook enters the meadow the sweet flag grows. In my boyhood there was a Shaker colony near by in New Hampshire and there one could buy candied sweet flag root. Whenever I see this plant I recall the austere stone buildings and the serious, hard-working Shakers, now long since departed.

I like, especially, to visit a marsh in fall.

122

It is a busy place. In the pool there's almost always a pair of hell-divers (or pied-billed grebes, if you prefer the book name), searching for late insects, leeches and minnows. Almost helpless on land and not much better aloft, hell-divers are masters of the water. With a little forward hop, they dive almost without a splash. Their reappearance is magical—"Now you don't see it, now you do!"

Song, and, occasionally, swamp sparrows are active in the rushes. A spotted sandpiper, no longer spotted in its winter clothing, bobs on a fallen log. Myrtle warblers flit through the willows in search of insects or pluck late fruits of the dogwoods.

Fall is house-building time for the muskrats. When you sit quietly by a marsh on a late fall afternoon, you're almost certain to see a muskrat sculling across the open water with a mouthful of cattails or grass roots, the building bricks of this rodent. The house, like a small haycock, may be difficult to see in the surrounding vegetation. By spring, however, it will be surrounded by a moat of open water after the 'rats have foraged beneath the ice for their winter food. (A muskrat house is shown on page 65.)

Examination of a mud flat reveals, by their tracks, that other creatures are busy in the marsh. Here you'll find the footprints of raccoon and deer, and perhaps those of a visiting porcupine seeking late water-lily pads. The small tracery of shrews' feet and the larger ones of meadow mice may be found. Relatives of the muskrat, the latter often make winter nests in the sides of their cousins' houses.

To my eye, reddish brown and orange-brown colors prevail in the dying marsh plants. The brilliant scarlet, vermilion and cardinal hues of the hillside maples, and the gold and lemon tints of willows, birches and poplars make a pleasing contrast with the soft tones of the marsh.

Against the snow of the winter marsh the stems of red osier stand out like veins. Only these and the tattered ladyfingers of the cattails relieve the white landscape. A shadow shows the location of the domed muskrat house. A closer look reveals that something has been going on there. Here, paired mink tracks weave in and out along the brook, then come directly to the house —and there they go on down the stream. But in between, the mink paused to dig out the meadow mouse's nest. A single bright drop of blood on the snow tells of a capture.

A sudden roaring whirr marks the departure of a grouse that had been feeding on poplar buds at the marsh-side. Now a flock of snow bunting drifts in to glean the few seeds of dock or smartweed extending above the snow. Except for those bits of life, the glacier has temporarily returned to the marsh.

My Life with the Porcupines

MIRIAM CHAPIN

GEORGE DALY Illustration

NOBODY WHO BUYS A VERMONT back-country farm and starts to live on it has to wait long for his first lesson in natural history. If he arrives in spring and leaves his car parked anywhere near the woods, he will receive his lesson the first morning, when he observes hunks bitten from his tires, and the remnants displaying marks of wide teeth. He may find that his horn won't blow, his lights won't go on. Chewed-up wiring can cost quite a lot to replace: porcupines are the greatest stimulant ever known to the purchase of fabricated garages—something that can be put up in a hurry. Maybe the manufacturers subsidize them. I wouldn't know, but I would believe anything about porcupines.

Or maybe the newcomer's registered poodle, all clipped and prancing, will come whining to his door with a sort of strange fringe, an unexpected gray mustache, around its muzzle. If he knows the woods, he knows there is just one thing to do, and that speed is of the essence. He sits down on the doorstep, yells for Tommy to bring the pliers, and holds the dog's head tight between his knees while he extracts the quills without regard for the anguished moans of poor Fido. Fido will learn, but his boss had better make a good job of his rude surgery, for a quill left in will fester, or even travel through flesh to eye or brain.

Like Fido, I had to learn. When I spent my first night in the old farmhouse I had bought, unoccupied for two years, I went to bed weary on a peaceful summer evening. It could not have been more than an hour or two later that I woke with a sawmill in full blast directly under my left ear. I sat up with a jump, scared at first and then realizing that the noise was not under the bed, but outside, under the window. I peered out, and there sat three large —at the moment they looked to me like grizzlies—grayish beasts, all chawing away mightily. They gazed at me serenely, not at all perturbed by this apparition in blue pajamas with a tousled mop of gray hair leaning above them. They did not appear to have any heads, only shiny shoe-button eyes at one end of round bodies. Then one of them rattled his quills disapprovingly and waddled off. I threw sticks of wood at the others until they too departed. But as soon as I went back to sleep they all came back, and by the noise they made they must have brought with them their sisters and their cousins and their aunts.

All that summer and indeed every summer since, my acquaintance with the porcupines progressed. I shot at them with an air gun, which annoyed but did not seriously discourage them. I induced a neighbor to kill two that insisted on roosting in the cellar, and I put wire netting over the windows. There were always one or two who loved the framework of my cellar windows, which seemed to have a specially attractive flavor, or the handle of any available shovel or hammer, where the human hand had given it a taste of salty sweat. And if you want a startling encounter, just open a woodshed door at black midnight and turn a flashlight on a big porcupine practically at your feet. He won't be disconcerted, but you will be.

Acting on learned advice, I put coarse salt on a log at the edge of the woods, and after that I could go out almost any night to find half a dozen feasting there. Some were little ones—for it seems that babies are born in spring, with their quills all flattened down like the down of baby chicks when they hatch, and like chicks they shake themselves dry and fluffy. They are not, however, exactly cuddlesome creatures, even when young. Nobody that I know of sends one for an Easter present. Their greatest usefulness might be as demonstration of the way to survive in a competitive world! Apparently salt is to them as cookie jar is to Junior. So long as I furnished salt, fewer came to chew on my car.

The Legislature of Vermont, I understand, at this writing [1958] is of two minds about porcupines. When they are plentiful, busily devouring cabins and chewing off spruce buds, it is inclined to regard them as a nuisance, and pay a bounty for tokens of their decease. When they are, for unknown reasons, scarcer, it thinks they should be protected to maintain the balance of wildlife. Or it wants to leave the decision to the foresters. In Canada it is argued that they must be preserved in spite of the trouble they make, because they have saved the life of more than one lost hunter, by being so easy to kill. Just a whack on the nose with a club will do the job. And then, rolled in clay and baked in the coals of a campfire, skin and quills coming off with the hard coating, they make good eating for a hungry man.

That I have never tried. It was a brilliant moonlight night, however, that I had my most thrilling adventure with the inhabitants of the woods about me. This time there was no sawmill under my bed. Instead I heard strange wailings and shriekings, hummings and singing, and a sort of sobbing cry. Bewildered, thinking some child must be in trouble somewhere, I got out of bed and went to the door. In the field behind the house, clear in the cool white light of an August moon, the porcupines were dancing. There were half a dozen of the prehistoric beasts, big ones and middle-sized ones, and they were certainly dancing.

No, I wasn't dreaming, nor had I had a drop to drink. I watched them. They shuffled about, they undulated like giant inchworms, they ran and jumped, they sashayed up to one another and retreated in a weird quadrille. All the time they sang loudly and mournfully, though I'm sure the occasion was a joyous one, a time of mating and celebration. The biggest one would prance up to a smaller one, I suppose his lady love, and adjure her in lyric tones to grant him her favor, and she would answer as if she were in deepest grief and amble away. I felt like Toomai of the Elephants, in the *Jungle Books* of my childhood—the little son of the elephant driver who rode one night on the back of the great Kala Nag to see the elephants dance in the far jungle, and grew up to be the only human being who ever lived to tell of that strange celebration.

I watched for more than an hour, until the first light of sunrise began to dim the moon, and one by one the queer specters trailed up the hill into the woods. After that, how could I bear to harm them? I feel I have been initiated into the tribe.

Spirit of the Forest

RONALD ROOD: *On the Hermit Thrush*

NO MATTER WHERE YOU GO IN Vermont in the summer, you're not far from the nearest woodland. Whether you work in the towns and cities, spend your days in the fields, or dream over a fishing rod, you are only a few minutes from one of the three and one-half million acres of forests of the Green Mountain State. And, in the cool part of the day at the edge of these woods, you can enjoy a privilege that comes to few Americans in a lifetime. You can hear one of the most haunting sounds in the wild—the bell-like note of the hermit thrush, Vermont's state bird.

This talented songster is common to all of Vermont's fourteen counties. Less frequent in southern New England, it nests in the northernmost states from Maine to Minnesota, as well as in southern Canada, and along mountains to Virginia. In our Green Mountain State, where it is particularly well known, farmers sometimes give it the unromantic name of "cow bird" or "chore bird" because it begins calling at chore-time in the afternoon. Of course the real cowbird is an entirely different creature, unable to sing an acceptable note and shunned by other birds for its habit of laying eggs in their nests.

Although you can hear the hermit thrush in almost any woodland—a long clear in-troductory note followed by four or five different-pitched phrases—you need patience to find it. Not only does it fall silent as you approach, but its brown coat blends with the leaves and underbrush. Even its white breast is dotted with brown, so it is easily mistaken for a patch of mottled sunlight under a spruce.

Once you see it, however, there's one identifying mark which sets it apart from other woodland birds—a rust-colored tail which it lifts sharply and then lets fall slowly—sometimes until it's almost vertical. As far as I can recall, there's no other New England bird with this trait.

The suggestion to adopt the hermit thrush as Vermont's official bird was made in the 1941 legislature. For a long time it had been informally so designated by the Vermont Federation of Women's Clubs. But when the bill was presented to make it legal, the legislators began to hedge on the question.

Some wanted the robin, but it was already the state bird elsewhere and had been proposed for another New England state (Connecticut, and adopted in 1943). Others suggested the well-known chickadee, as it didn't leave with the coming of cold weather like the thrush and robin, but stayed in Vermont the year round. However, Maine had adopted the chickadee back in 1927. Pennsylvania had spoken for the ruffed grouse, or "partridge." Someone else suggested the blue jay, one of the most rugged and down-to-earth birds, which could be seen all year and which brought the color of the blue sky to the wintry landscape. Besides, no nearby state had claimed it for its own.

This triggered still another suggestion. "If you've got to have a bird that's a rugged individualist," it was argued, "one that's around all the time, and one that nobody else has—then, how about the crow?"

Now this threw attention back to the original bill. It was brought to a vote. The retiring little thrush, unaware of all the stir, prevailed by a narrow margin. As one member of that 1941 legislature told me when I asked him what he could recall about it, "as I remember, the aye's were just a little above the no's."

Actually, the hermit thrush blends the qualities of the two main groups of residents who make up Vermont today. It is both a native Vermonter and a summer visitor. Although it leaves for the southern half of the United States with the approach of cold weather, it was hatched and raised in Vermont. And, like so many other Vermonters, it can never break the ties with its native region. It comes back in April of each succeeding year.

Although the hermit thrush is as solitary as its name implies, you may think you're looking at a robin out of place when you finally get a glimpse of it. It hops along the ground like a robin looking for worms, although it prefers the lower branches of trees. It builds a bowl-shaped nest of twigs and moss like a robin's, but without mud as a cement. Its three to five eggs are almost robin's-egg blue in color. In fact, the two birds are closely related, as the speckled breast of a fledgling robin plainly shows.

The thrush, however, is only two-thirds the size of its larger cousin.

It has several other Vermont relatives. All of them are gifted singers. You may have heard the wood thrush, whose song has been likened to a rising succession of bells. It is a bird with large spots and a reddish cast about the head. The veery, or Wilson's thrush, sings in a breezy whistle of several descending notes. It has small indistinct spots on the breast, and is a general tawny color. The olive-backed, and the similar gray-cheeked, thrush are less common; their color is indicated by their name. But the hermit thrush is the only thrush with a solid reddish tail distinctly different in color from its back.

One more member completes the family as it is seen in Vermont. This is the bluebird—the welcome visitor whose liquid warble is heard from a fencepost or tree stub as early as March. It, too, is a thrush. So is the world's most celebrated singer, the nightingale. Thus Vermont's state bird is in royal company.

One June day I was walking through the sugar woods behind my home in Lincoln. A pair of hermit thrushes flew around me in distress. I knew by the short low "chuck" note that their nest was close by.

I picked my way carefully over the ground lest I step on the nest. Suddenly, less than a foot away from my shoe, four heads snapped up as if on springs. Four red mouths opened wide in a request for food. The parents became frantic and flew within a few feet of me, making a commotion in an attempt to lure me away from their blind, naked young.

I noted the spot—next to the base of an old beech stump. Then I continued on my way. But a few days later the babies were gone. Perhaps a fox, following my footprints, had discovered them. But all through July the male continued to sing, so I knew

128

that the undaunted parents had built an-other nest near by. I hoped that the ap-proximate month from egg-laying to first solo flight had been safer this time.

The Indians appreciated the clear tones of the hermit thrush, and passed down a legend as to how it got its song. The Great Spirit put all the birds and animals on the earth to make their way as best they could. Soon many of them began to complain and squabble with their neighbors. But the her-mit thrush stole into the solitude of the forest and set about the task which it con-tinues today—the eating of tremendous quantities of harmful insects.

The Great Spirit, tired of listening to the arguments of the other creatures, went into the forest to rest. Not a bug or a beetle was to be seen. Instead, the somber-colored thrush was quietly searching the undergrowth for insects.

In gratitude for this service and for its contentment with its lot, the Great Spirit reached forth his hand. Immediately the woods rang with music as the voiceless thrush burst into its exquisite song.

Sometimes that song continues all day during rainy weather. And the thrush may be heard long after the sun has set and every other bird has been stilled. Campers sometimes hear it in the middle of the night like its European cousin, the night-ingale.

No sound in the woods is more emblem-atic of the peace and serenity of the Ver-mont forests in summer than that of *Hylo-cichla guttata:* the "spotted spirit of the woodland."

Whistle-Pig

RONALD ROOD: *On Woodchucks*

ROBERT CANDY Illustrations

OUR OLD GERMAN SHEPHERD WAS able to lick nearly everything in the neighborhood. This included cats, most other dogs, and even, on one memorable occasion, a skunk. But he met his match in a waddling, grizzled-red woodchuck which took up residence in our pasture.

Day after day Fritz tried to catch the big rodent unawares. Finally he got his chance. Seeing the 'chuck an unusual distance from the earth mound that marked the entrance to his hole, Fritz raced toward him. Triumphantly touching the mound like a baserunner rounding first, he galloped off toward his victim. It looked bad for the woodchuck, which stood rooted to the spot.

Fritz launched himself and landed perfectly on target. Only the target wasn't there any more. With a saucy whistle, the 'chuck did a turnabout and disappeared—down a hole we didn't even know existed.

Fritz was caught up so short that he stubbed his nose. Then he began to dig frantically. The whistle-pig's bolt hole, carefully dug from beneath so no telltale earth would show, began to look like a disaster area as dirt flew in a shower.

An hour later the dog stopped to rest. Then the 'chuck delivered the final blow. His bolt hole, of course, connected with several tunnels running along two feet beneath the surface. One of them led to the main entrance some thirty feet away. Now he sat up in this entrance and whistled. He leisurely scratched a flea. Then, a split second ahead of the enraged Fritz, he did his disappearing act again.

That did it. Fritz sniffed in disgust. "You don't play fair," his manner plainly said as he gave up and headed for the house.

As I recall, Fritz never bothered that 'chuck again. Although he continued to insist on lordship of our little farm, he allowed the woodchuck his fifty yards of clover and weeds, and occasional snail or insect tidbits.

Anyone who knows 'chucks would probably not be surprised at this turn of events. For woodchucks have a way of coming out on top. I recall my first trip over a section of Interstate Highway 89. The snorting road machinery had just recently left the great double ribbons of pavement, and we were among the first cars to try it out. But the woodchucks had already moved in. Heedless of the cars racing along within a few feet, there'd be one every few miles, munching placidly on vetch or dandelion greens—or on the new grass which had been thoughtfully planted right where it was handiest.

In fact, this roly-poly ground squirrel

(for that's really what it is) along almost any highway in the northern two-thirds of our United States and Canada, is a real tourist attraction. As it sits up straight like a portly picket pin or grazes like a complacent little cow, it will catch the eye of everybody in the car.

If it's a small, five-pound female, it will probably be tabbed as a woodchuck. However, if it happens to be a two-foot male of, say, a whopping ten or twelve pounds, it may prompt all kinds of excited guesses. If it dives across the road ahead in a ripple of fur, fat and muscle with its six-inch hairy tail in a low arch, it's likely to turn into a beaver, raccoon or bear cub by the time the travelers decide what it was.

Life for the big rodent begins in a grass-lined underground nest. A friend of mine turned over such a nest early in May when digging a ditch.

"There were five young in it," he recalled. "They were about four inches long, bare-naked, and blind as a litter of puppies. We fed them warm milk with a medicine dropper. They finally got little fur coats and opened their eyes when they were about a month old."

In the wild, the woodchuck kits are weaned at five or six weeks. Then they go on the diet that serves them for the rest of their lives—almost anything that grows. Tumbling out ahead of the mother in the early morning dew, they often wrestle and play like kittens.

By mid-July their enthusiasm for life has taken them in different directions. Each one builds its own little burrow—near the top of a hillside, at the base of a stump, or sometimes under a ledge. They are neat in their personal habits, so they dig a separate chamber for their toilet needs. They periodically cover the waste with fresh dirt.

From then until autumn their days are mainly composed of eating, napping, and

not getting caught at either. Besides sharp-shooting farm boys and their dogs, they have to watch for foxes and an occasional ambitious hawk. By late September or October they're ready for a four or five months' snooze.

"Did your 'chucks go dormant in the fall?" I asked my friend.

"No," he answered. "But they sure ate as if they were going to. I'd given away all but two of them by August, and I'm glad I did. They spent half the day mowing our lawn like a couple of little sheep. When they started on our dahlias and lilies, we put them in a pen. We found they liked oatmeal and bread, so we fed them until they were almost too fat to walk. I'm told they eat like this in the wild, too. I guess it helps them get ready for winter. But they never went to sleep. Probably the kids played with them too much."

Why woodchucks suddenly cease to feed just when the fall rains are making everything green is somewhat of a mystery. Probably, it has to do with decreasing length of daylight. Right in the midst of plenty, they just stop eating. Then for several days they wander about while their digestive tract empties itself.

Ready at last, each 'chuck retires to a leafy nest underground. Plugging and tamping and sealing itself in with dirt, it

curls up and drops into slumber. Deeper and deeper it sleeps as the hours pass until it's in that mysterious almost-death that is hibernation.

Curled up, its head tucked down until its nose touches its belly, it seems to "freeze" into a hard ball. Body temperature, normally about that of a human, plummets to a chilly forty degrees or less. Breathing slows from thirty-five times a minute to once in five minutes. The heart beats only a few times per minute—so slowly that the blood pools up in internal organs, and a wound does not bleed. Then, with its fires banked low, the woodchuck waits beneath the frostline while the winter's blizzards rage above it.

In spite of this profound slumber, it takes only an hour to awaken. Once at college I watched a 'chuck in the process. His toes twitched and his eyes tried to open. I put my hand gently on his coarse-furred body and could feel his pulse and breathing rate increase by the minute. Smacking his lips and yawning, he struggled himself awake. Getting to his feet, he staggered around the cage.

"Looks the way you do after the alarm goes off," grinned my roommate.

Some woodchucks apparently have insomnia, just as people do. They may poke out of hiding at any time; I have seen them on a January day, trying to graze on a patch of dead grass. It is this midwinter appearance, probably, that gives rise to the Groundhog Day tradition, for groundhogs are nothing but woodchucks.

Like people also, 'chucks are unpredictable. Occasionally they go on the night shift. We've watched them through binoculars in a moonlit meadow. We've found them up ahead of us when we arose early to go bird-watching. And a rare groundhog hearkens back to its dim squirrel past as it climbs a tree to escape an enemy or just to sun itself. Then, squirrel-like, it descends the tree headfirst—something not even the arboreal porcupine can do.

It can swim, too. That jelly-roll body floats well. A naturalist has followed one across the Mississippi where the river was half a mile wide. Another 'chuck lived in a riverbank and crossed a forty-foot stream daily for food. It's this lure of the other side, perhaps, that leads them to dash across the road in front of your car.

Many a farmer has gone on the warpath after he's dropped a tractor wheel into a hidden 'chuck hole or sliced off the top of a stony mound with his mower. Horses and cows have been known to break legs when they stepped into a burrow. But there's a plus side to the story. It came to me vividly after a forest fire.

I was poking through the rubble of a twenty-acre burn. It had been a fierce little fire. Sadly I nudged the carcass of a raccoon which had been driven out of its hollow tree. Something made me look at the ground to my left. There, although it was a hundred feet into the woods, was the familiar mound and hole of a woodchuck. And peering out at me were four pairs of frightened little eyes. As I looked, I could pick out the black-masked faces of four baby raccoons which had found shelter there.

Since then I've learned that woodchucks *do* go into woods more than people suspect. Sometimes a meadow burrow will have a bolt hole fifty feet away in a woodland. Such holes are used in the nick of time by many a frantic refugee.

Like a man who finds a whole new list of friends when he installs a swimming pool, the woodchuck's burrow gives him a host of neighbors. Skunks, rabbits, southern opossums, turtles, snakes and foxes are apt to move in. Philosophically, he just digs more burrows, although he could defend his rights well with those white chisel-teeth —as more than one farm dog has found out to its sorrow.

"Their half-acre becomes a one-'chuck wildlife refuge," a New York game warden told me. "A few years back there was a county-wide extermination campaign where I grew up. Farmers and sportsmen gathered together to poison the holes with gas and clean up the woodchuck nuisance.

"Like so many attempts to tinker with nature, it backfired," he continued. "There was such a howl from the skunk trappers who found their fur crop cut in half, and from the rabbit hunters who couldn't find a target, that the authorities had to reverse themselves. They slapped legal protection on the woodchuck, and it became against the law to molest them. Now Wisconsin and a few other states protect them, even though you don't in Vermont."

The Algonkian Indians also had a high opinion of the woodchuck. They called it "we-jack," from which we get its most common name today. It made an interesting camp pet. Stewed or roasted, with the glands removed from its forelegs so it didn't taste so musky, it was served to guests as a special treat.

The Chippewas called it "kuk-wah-geeser." French Canadians, hearing its shrill, penetrating whistle, call it "le siffleur"—the whistler. Scientists have named it *Marmota monax*, recalling its relationship to the other marmots and ground squirrels. Farmers call it whistle-pig, moonack, groundhog, or several less printable names when it takes up engineering or grocery-shopping in their meadows and gardens.

But old whistle-pig doesn't care. He just waddles along, eating crabgrass or corn with equal gusto. If we insist on tearing up his woods and brushlands and planting a fine garden of tasty beans and peas, that's all right with him.

He'll just take it in stride. Plant by plant and row by row.

Woodland's Beating Heart

RONALD ROOD: *On the Ruffed Grouse*

EDWARD J. BRUNDAGE Illustration

SHE FLUTTERED DOWN THE TRAIL, whining piteously like a puppy. One brown wing hung uselessly, and her left leg seemed hardly able to support her body. Her splendid tail, spread fanwise, dragged in the dust.

"Ruffed grouse," I grinned to allay my companion's concern. "And I bet she thinks she's fooling us with that broken-wing act. Ten to one she's got a bunch of chicks somewhere. If we move we'll probably step on one."

He hardly glanced at the mottled bird five feet in front of us. Instead, he squatted down and peered at the leaves.

Now she changed her tactics—so suddenly that we both stepped back. Hissing, she rushed at us, her "broken wing" forgotten. Her feathers fluffed until she looked twice her size. Stamping her feet, she pulled up short just a few inches away. No mother hen ever looked more defiant.

Warily, we bent over again, with one eye on the belligerent grouse. We could see nothing but dry leaves in the rut made by a sap-gathering sled toward the end of sugaring several weeks before. I was carrying a willow switch and idly I poked it at a brown bug that had stirred on the surface of a leaf. The bug disappeared.

I looked closer. The "bug" was there again. It was no bug at all, but a twinkling eye. And the "leaf" was a brown-black downy chick, scarcely larger than a ping-pong ball. Crouched against the earth, it blended perfectly. Only its eye movement had given it away.

The dangers that beset the creature known locally as a "partridge" are fantastic. The nest, scooped out at the base of a stump or log, is a welcome find for skunks, foxes, squirrels, and even chipmunks. These last apparently think the one-and-three-quarter-inch eggs are some new species of nut, for the they carefully hide them in their storehouses. Later, after the babies hatch, a single downpour may blur out the lives of an entire brood if they get chilled and drenched before they can run under their mother's wing. And at every instant they must watch for danger from the air, the trees, the ground.

Their numbers are reduced in many ways. Several years ago I found a mass of feathers under a tree. An owl, searching for mice, had come across a bonanza in the form of roosting grouse. The house cat gone wild, one of the most predatory creatures in the woods, takes more. Forest fires pay no heed to a mother feigning a broken wing; nests of roasted eggs are sometimes found, with the bones of the mother a few feet away.

Babies become blinded and weakened by lice and mites, and disease or enemies soon finish them off. Blackhead, a fatal virus disease of turkeys and chickens, sometimes

rampages through a forest full of grouse. A brood that averages six chicks in June will be cut in half in July; by late August only two will be left.

A few days before the first spring flowers appear, the cock grouse finds a fallen log in the forest. He seems quite fussy about this; the log must be about one foot through or larger, and partially screened by bushes. Rarely, he settles for the exposed root of a large tree, but one thing seems sure: no logs or roots, then no cock grouse—and hence no "partridge" in the woods.

Then starts one of nature's thrilling displays. Although he weighs but a pound and a half, he fluffs up his feathers like a little turkey. That black-bordered tail fans out and the wings project down at his sides. The metallic-black ruff spreads like an Elizabethan collar. His brown topknot rises like the crest of a jay.

Back and forth he patters on the log, turning this way and that. He hisses with a noise described by the late Arthur Allen of Cornell as similar to briskly rubbing the sleeve or the trouser leg.

Then the strutting stops. He takes a position crossways to the log. Rising up, tail pressing down against the log, he flaps his wings forward and upward. Thump!—the compression of the stroke makes a beat in the air. Thump! Another beat half a second later, as the air is again compressed. Then thump—thump—thump—thump-thumprrrrrrr-*thump* as the beats come faster and faster, ending with a drumlike roll. The whole tattoo takes about ten seconds.

Scarcely louder at close quarters than at several hundred feet, the sound is felt as much as it is heard. It can be noted half a mile away. Edward Howe Forbush, the Massachusetts naturalist, called it "the muffled beating of a great heart." The Indians called the grouse the "carpenter bird" because they thought the noise was made as its wings struck the log like a hammer. But Dr. Allen's motion pictures of a grouse drumming show that it strikes nothing but air.

You can approximate this sound by beating your chest. Try it sometime in the woods—when nobody is looking. If you're fortunate, you may hear an answering roll. For the drum of the grouse is apparently a challenge to other males, just as the strutting is for the benefit of some little lady who comes to the vicinity of the log ostensibly in search of buds and green leaves. A drumming male lays claim to about four acres of woodland and a single mate, although it's suspected that sometimes he may have more than one wife. In fact, there are cases where two females have sat on the same nest at once.

He cannot stand the presence of another male. Grouse have been known to attack one-lung tractors, apparently in the mistaken belief that their pop-pop-pop represents some monstrous interloper. I have heard of a grouse-fight started by an observer who drummed on his chest until two males came to the spot and pitched into each other.

Occasionally it is possible to sneak up on a drumming male, he's so intent at his task. You may even be lucky enough to sit on the other end of the log and watch him. But by late June or July he falls silent, although in autumn he may reminisce at his favorite log. Sometimes he's answered by an adolescent son across the valley.

If success attends his springtime drumming efforts, the male finds that he has company. It is in the form of a brownish female, almost identical in appearance to the male, but with little of his boldness. She seems quite timid and afraid. With all the forest to be afraid in, though, she chooses to show her timidity just a few feet away from the male. Of course, this spurs him on—until, finally, after much strutting and drumming, he wins his mate.

The female lays her buff-colored eggs in May—one a day, as a chicken does. She sits on them for about three weeks. Blending perfectly with the forest floor, she often adds to the concealment by covering herself with leaves and grass. Then, as she steals away to feed, the leaves slide off and hide the eggs. The young, scarcely half the size of baby chicks, hatch in late May. They can walk minutes after they are born.

In ten days their little wing feathers are strong enough for them to fly. The first grouse family I ever saw as a boy astonished me by taking to the trees. There they teetered, looking down at me while the female uttered her nervous "quit-quit." They looked like fluffy, tailless sparrows.

All summer the feathers develop, while the young wander through the brushland and second-growth woods. The family fans out in front of the mother like an amoeba spreading, foraging slowly, devouring insects, wild strawberries and other fruit. They keep in touch by quiet little calls. They seldom see their father, although he may join them in the fall. By late September they are nearly full grown, and mottled brown or gray, with barred breasts.

The Indians called the autumn months the "crazy moon." They noticed the strange antics of some grouse at this time. One October day I was driving through Hinesburg when a feathered bullet hurtled through the air a few feet in front of me. Then it crashed into the side of a building.

I stopped my car and knelt beside the grouse. Dazed but still game, it fearlessly surveyed me. I could see the beginning of the feathered "stockings" which would develop along the shinbone for protection during the winter. Its toes were edged with newly formed "snowshoes"—temporary, comblike projecting scales enabling it to walk on the soft snow.

I reached out to stroke it. Little gamecock that it was, it delivered a resounding peck with its beak. Fluttering to its senses, it took off with a roar of wings. I watched as it veered to left and right, crashing through the branches of an elm and sailing out across a meadow.

No one can explain the "crazy flight." No one, either, has explained self-tamed grouse, which sometimes follow campers like pets.

Nor has there been a good explanation for the "grouse-cycle." This is a population build-up of about ten years: then there's a sudden crash of numbers with only a few left. Cold, wet springs have been suggested as a cause. So have been parasites, disease and the deadly sleet storms, when the winter supply of buds and twigs is coated with ice. Perhaps it's a combination of a number of factors. The cycle seems to operate throughout most of the grouse's range, from Pennsylvania to Oregon, south along the mountains, and north into Canada and Alaska. Many wildlife managers suggest a closed season on hunting at the "low" of the cycle to help the grouse recover.

Once you hear the thunder of a grouse taking off through the woods, you'll not forget it. The bird rises so violently that it stirs up a cloud of leaves and dust in its wake. Then it flicks its wings saucily as it sets for a triumphant glide into a thicket.

It was not always this wary. At one time it was called "fool hen," not only because of its chickenlike appearance but because it placed its trust in man, even allowing itself to be killed with a stick. A century ago it sold at eight for a dollar in Boston. Since then it has learned to protect itself. Now it quickly puts a tree or bush between itself and danger as it flies, and is gone in a moment. Pursued by a hawk or day-flying owl in winter, it may dive into a snowdrift, where it burrows several feet horizontally before it emerges in full flight. It's been known to plummet into water, for it can even swim if necessary.

Often in the winter we find a hole in our woods where a grouse has plunged into the snow for a cozy nap. Next morning it bursts out again—unless a rare ice storm traps it beneath the crust. Foxes sometimes pounce on the hole, but usually come up with only a mouth full of snow. The wily grouse tunnels two or three feet to one side before settling down.

Look for *Bonasa umbellus,* whose name means "grouse of the shade," in overgrown woodlots and openings in the forest during the summer. Catch your breath as it explodes from a thicket of beeches, oaks, hawthorns, sumacs and other seed-producers in the fall. Find it in mixed hardwoods and evergreens in winter, feeding on poplar, birch and wild apple buds. See it gathering roadside grit to help its gizzard crush food. Discover it under a January moon, snug against the trunk of a hemlock or other evergreen while frost forms around its nostrils and the maples crack with the cold.

Occasionally you will even see it in a cornfield near the woods, or sampling the edge of a buckwheat patch. But you'll seldom find it cooped up on a game farm like a pheasant or quail, for later release. Although it has been raised experimentally, it seldom can abide too close contact with man. It lives its wild life magnificently, at top speed. As one old-timer told me, almost reverently:

"There ain't a finer bird in the woods."

The Quick Red Fox

RONALD ROOD

ROBERT CANDY Illustration

HE'S BEEN KNOWN TO JUMP INTO a picnic fireplace when hard pressed, or to run through a herd of cows.

On one occasion, he added a new note to a church service as he dashed through the open door.

His ability to outwit his enemies is so well known that "crafty as a fox" is about as smart as an animal can get. Yet my neighbor on the hill has had one jump recklessly out of the roadside bushes at him, barking like a little dog.

"That red fox sure didn't show much caution. If I'd had a stick I could have clobbered him. He kept jumping up and down and barking that sharp little bark. He was so close that I could see the catlike pupils of his eyes. It made me nervous, to say the least, because a fox can have rabies.

"I looked around for something to use for a weapon in case he attacked. Then I saw what his trouble was. Sitting by a stump were three little pups. Big black ears pricked up, cute as they could be. They were so interested in their father's antics that they forgot to hide. No wonder daddy fox was upset. He chased me clear down the road."

There are plenty of tales of the sacrifices made by animals for their young. But, like almost anything else you could name, the red fox may go them one better. Many a woodsman has known of a young, inexperienced fox which was almost run to earth by an enemy until its mother dashed ahead of the very jaws of death at the last moment. Then, while her little one got a much-needed rest, she soon led her tracker harmlessly away.

Life begins for this sharp-faced little wild dog early in April. From four to nine blind, helpless kits are born in an abandoned woodchuck burrow or beneath the roots of an old stump. New England's rocky soil being what it is, and foxes being somewhat less than enthusiastic about digging dens of their own, the same spot may be used for years. Also, more than one vixen may occupy the same burrow. However, marital lines are strictly drawn; foxes apparently have one mate for life or at least for the current season.

After three weeks, the kits begin to appear at the entrance to the den. They romp like puppies. Oddly, the den entrance is usually exposed for all to see. For several summers there was one a few hundred feet from the front of Brown's General Store in Lincoln. The village people often watched the pups playing up on the hill right in broad daylight. When visitors asked what they were, they didn't believe it when told they were real wild foxes.

At first the dog (male) fox does most of the grocery shopping. He is joined by the vixen as the family gets older. As the kits growl and pull at the food, the ground becomes a regular playpen, strewn with bones and litter. Then the parents begin to drop food a little distance away so the kits have to search for it. Finally the return of the parents is a signal for a regular little hunting party. Thus the kits rehearse for the same thing in the real life that soon will follow.

By late summer the kits are quite well grown. They begin to trade the woolly, light, puppy fur for the glossy, dense coat of the adult. The black "stockings" they wore as babies are somewhat less conspicuous.

Although the usual color of *Vulpes fulva* is reddish yellow or fulvous above (hence its name), and whitish beneath, there are many variations. One kit may be a normal color while its litter-mate may be a "cross-fox" (red-brown with black on the shoulders). There is also a yellow fox, of a tawny lion color. The rare black fox is merely a valuable color mutation, while the silver and platinum are most prized of all.

The highest price ever paid for a skin of

any kind in this country was eleven thousand dollars—for a single platinum fox skin. And a breeding pair of silver foxes once went for thirty-five thousand. Of course you don't see fur prices like that any more. And most fox pelts are ranch-raised, because they can be taken in their prime.

As soon as it gets its dense winter coat, the red fox begins an almost endless struggle—to keep it on its own shoulders. For years the little ten- to fourteen-pounder has been the quarry of tons of hunters, hounds and horses. Nor does it always come out second best. On one celebrated hunt, one hundred marksmen took part. Result: two men hit, not a fox touched. On another, nine hounds were lost when the fox made a sharp U-turn at the edge of a cliff.

Add to these an irate poultry farmer with a shotgun, a trapper with his careful "fox sets" and a farm dog out to show who's boss, and you can see why a fox which lives more than ten years is a real old-timer. Vermont has no closed season except for pursuit with dogs.

"They get as much fun out of life as any animal I know, even if everybody's against them," a fur dealer told me. "They will make a fancy trail for a dog to follow—up on fences, down the middle of streams, apparently through culverts although they've really jumped up on top. Sometimes they'll cover twenty miles. Then they'll circle back to watch the dog at work.

"I used to make my rounds by horse and buggy in the old days," he continued. "There was a little fox that always followed me for about a mile, probably about the limit of his own home territory. When I stopped, he'd stop. When I started up, he did the same. Like a little shadow. Or like a little dog. Maybe the first pet dog of a caveman was a sort of wild fox."

Doglike, too, the creature that the French trappers called Renard often visits clumps of grass and fenceposts, leaving a spot of urine as a memento of his passing. The next fox to come along dutifully adds his own scent to the community bulletin board, and so on. Musky glands at the base of the tail supply further odor. Sometimes farm dogs will follow a fox trail, investigating each signpost and solemnly joining the club in turn. In fact, there are cases of actual friendships built up between Rover and Renard. Apparently, however, no fox-dog litters have ever been proven.

Foxes have been known to play with cattle in the fields. They run around and around just inside the fence, with the cattle after them. The cattle could run faster and so could the fox. It seems to be just a game on both parts.

Admittedly the red fox sometimes enters the farmyard for a less commendable purpose. Finding a trove of a hundred sleeping chickens or turkeys, it finds itself unable to resist. The next day the farmer is on the warpath to avenge a dozen hens. Soon the red fox finds a price on its head.

Several states (including Vermont from 1890-1906) have placed bounties on foxes. Often the reward is paid when the claimant presents a fox tail to the town authorities as evidence of a kill. However, bounties have been less than successful on several counts. First, overenthusiastic hunters sometimes forget state boundaries and bring in fox tails from a state which doesn't pay a bounty to a state which does. Second, farseeing characters would cruelly cut the tail or brush from a captive fox. Then the forty-inch fox—now only about two feet long—ran off to raise more foxes, complete with tails.

Third, bounties aren't that simple an answer to overproduction. "In Wisconsin, where bounties have been in effect for seventy-five years, foxes are as prevalent as ever," a county agent informed me. "In the

South, fox-control campaigns have turned out to be quail-control campaigns, too—by mistake.

"Foxes hold down rats and mice which, in turn, eat the eggs of ground-nesting birds. Here in Vermont, mice in a meadow eat standing hay. They eat corn in a cornfield. They girdle young apple trees in winter. And a fox will eat a mouse every chance it gets."

A friend told me of watching a distant fox at a mouse nest. "It held its pose for so long that I began to doubt it was a fox at all," he said. "It must have been there for fifteen minutes with one leg raised, poised over that clump of grass. Then it jumped right onto the nest like a flash. It was just waiting for that mouse to make a false move."

Foxes stalk grasshoppers like a cat during their infrequent daytime jaunts, for they'd rather hunt at night. They relish beechnuts, acorns and almost every kind of berry that Vermont produces. They love rabbits, squirrels, chipmunks, woodchucks. Once I saw a flock of pigeons craning their necks out in the middle of a cornfield. There lay a fox as if dead at the base of a corn shock, just waiting for one to come too close. And, in spite of Aesop, they love grapes—sour or not.

For years, the red fox has been kept in check by wolves, coyotes, lynx and bobcats. It also seldom visits the deep forests. Here in Vermont, however, we're short on all the predators named except the bobcat. And we've carefully provided lots of open areas —second-growth brush and abandoned farms—which are just to the fox's liking.

Trapping pressure has let up, too, with wild pelts seldom worth the taking. Add to this an ability to get along even within city limits (it's been recorded from New York, Chicago and Boston), and one can easily understand why the red fox's recorded range takes in all of North America except for the deserts, and southeastern and western coasts.

With living conditions this perfect, something has to step in, or we'd be overrun with foxes. One powerful check is in the form of a tiny mite. This almost microscopic creature burrows beneath the skin, causing mange. Two years ago I picked up a red fox in Starksboro, blind, starved and almost hairless with the disease. As it passes by contact, mange weakens the fox and other diseases quickly cut big populations down to size.

Renard is full grown by the time he is six months old. Then the family breaks up. The fox lives a solitary existence, sleeping almost anywhere the mood strikes him, until some time in February. Then one night his yapping bark will be answered by the cry of the vixen, which has been likened to "the agonized scream of a demented woman." Family duties will begin about fifty-one days later.

In summer the fox grows fat on all manner of meats and vegetables, often burying what he cannot eat and returning to it later. In winter he will dig for frozen apples, or pounce on a grouse sleeping buried on a snowdrift, or lie in wait for a snowshoe hare. He may even stuff his stomach with gravel and sticks when the eating is poor.

If a dog comes snooping too close, the light-footed fox may lay a careful trail over the thin ice of a nearby stream. Then while his pursuer flounders in the frigid water, he finds a snowdrift and curls around and around until he makes his bed. Carefully he lays that warm, insulating brush over his paws and sensitive nose while his big cousin takes his dampened enthusiasm homeward.

141

Let all your senses tell you of Autumn...

RONALD ROOD

MY DOG STOPPED IN HIS TRACKS, one foot raised. He waited with ears erect, every muscle tense.

I stopped, too, and strained my eyes to see what had caught his attention.

Ahead of us a little pile of leaves suddenly flew apart. Bounding out of them came a striped chipmunk, his cheeks stuffed with beechnuts. A month earlier we would probably have passed him unnoticed. The green plants and decaying mold of the forest floor would have muffled the sound of his activity. Now, however, the new crop of fallen leaves betrayed his slightest move.

This is the way with an autumn walk. New sounds and new senses are at every hand, and old ones are magnified. A white-footed mouse bounding through the leaves sounds like a deer. The crisp air brings sounds from astonishing distances—the slamming of a faraway door, or the call of unseen crows. Perhaps you may hear the postseason drumming of a ruffed grouse on a log, so distant that all you do is feel the beat of the powerful wings and cannot tell the direction of the sound.

In the meadows of autumn, you can hear a population explosion. Most of the grasshoppers, crickets and katydids have been silent until now. They couldn't have made a noise if they'd wanted to. They've merely been awkward, growing nymphs whose wings or legs or other organs of sound-production have been slow to develop. Now with the shedding of the last juvenile skin, a million adolescents emerge as adults.

Generally it's the males that sing, proclaiming their new status from a blade of grass or sprig of goldenrod. Their numbers swell with each new arrival until, in September, the countryside is a big insect hubbub.

"How can I catch 'em?" wailed one small friend who went out into the insect din in our meadow to find a katydid. "I don't know where to look. I hear them everywhere!"

During the sunny part of the day, the insect chorus races headlong. But if the weather turns cool, so does the enthusiasm of the songsters. They sing at a slower pace. And on a night that hovers near frost, only a few crickets scratch out a slow cadence with their wings. Finally, they, too, fall silent.

There is one familiar insect so delicately tuned to the weather that you can tell the temperature merely by listening to its song. This is the snowy tree-cricket. It's a nocturnal, greenish-white insect about an inch long with a medium-pitched, pleasantly musical note. You may hear the tree-cricket from a bush or tree trunk—sometimes dozens of them in unison.

Once you've identified the tune, you're ready for the temperature. Count the number of chirps in fifteen seconds. Add forty, and there's your answer in degrees. It's surprisingly accurate, too.

The insect songsters are as typical of autumn as the birds are typical of summer or the chorus of frogs is of spring. But on a frosty morning the insects are silent. Almost all frosty mornings are clear and still in Vermont, for it's the absence of cloud cover that lets the heat escape from the earth. With the rising of the sun, however, there's a new autumn sound. We often go

outside just before sunrise to hear it.

The sound begins as the first rays of the sun stretch to our maples. At first we hear only a faint whisper. Then there's another whisper—and another, until it sounds as if we're standing in the middle of a ghostly waterfall. Only this is a *leaf*-fall—the parting of leaves from the tree as the last few cells of the leafstalks give way under the combination of frost and sun. In a matter of minutes, a huge tree may shed almost all its leaves without a breath of wind. As you watch, it may cover the ground with a red-and-yellow carpet where half an hour before there was but frosted grass.

Out in the meadow, you may hear other frosty-sunny sounds. They come in an irregular snapping, like the crackling of an invisible fire. Seed pods of weeds, split by the frost, fly open at the touch of the sun's rays, throwing their burdens in all directions. The purple vetch is especially good at this: its pods split with a corkscrew twist, making a sound like elfin fingers snapping.

Go to the edge of the woods and you'll hear more cracklings. Witch-hazel capsules, bearing their loads of little seeds, grow in such a way that tensions build up along the capsules' seams. Under the action of frost and sun, the seams finally spring open. This throws the seeds as much as twenty feet in all directions, like miniature popcorn. You can hear a witch-hazel bush "explode" many yards away. The tiny seeds falling on the leaves sound like a small sleet storm.

"There was another sound," a Bennington resident recalled, "which I haven't heard for years. Frost would open the chestnut burrs and we'd hear the nuts fall to the ground in the woods. Today, the chestnut is gone. But you can still hear the sound of falling beechnuts, hickory nuts and acorns—that is, the ones the squirrels haven't gotten."

One October day Peg and I stopped by the side of a country road. We turned off the engine, got out and leaned against the fender. As we stood there, a noise seemed to come and go on the breeze. It sounded like dozens of rusty hinges creaking and squawking high in the sky.

We looked up. Perhaps half a mile above our heads, stretched out in a thin wavering V, was a flock of more than a hundred Canada geese. The old gander, whose wings cleft the air at its point, stretched his neck toward the south. Some scientists say that geese fly in formation so that only one wing beats the unbroken air. Others say it's an aerial version of the "single file" for which geese are noted on the ground. But no matter what the explanation, a sight such as the one we watched and listened to will be remembered a lifetime. More important, we would have missed it completely if we had stayed in the car. By habit, man seldom raises his eyes more than fifteen degrees above the horizon.

There's another autumn sensation, too. Put on a blindfold so you cannot see the fall colors. Stuff your ears with cotton so you aren't able to hear the autumn sounds. You will still be able to guess the season. Your nose will give you a clue. Poor though our sense of smell may be, it still brings us the messages of fall.

Drive slowly along a Vermont road. A faint winey smell tells you of wild grapes in a fencerow. You catch the scent of asters fading on a hillside. You get the pungent smell of ferns touched by frost. There are chokecherries, smelling something like bitter almonds; sumac with its lemony aroma. There's the rich smell of goldenrod, unjustly blamed by many hay fever sufferers for their woes, while its cousin, ragweed, goes almost unnoticed.

Then, of course, there's the aroma of burning leaves. "Doesn't really make sense to burn them," a county agent told me. "Besides the fire hazard, burning leaves release all the mineral matter back to the soil at once—too fast for the new growth to use it all. And the organic matter goes up in smoke. But I suppose people will keep right on burning them." And so they probably will, if for no other reason than that burning leaves smell so good.

The sounds and smells of an autumn in Vermont are there for the savoring as much as the autumn sights themselves—the flaming foliage, the clear mountain air, the golden days.

"I guess it's like the man who had a captive eagle," a photographer mused as we considered the limitations of even the finest color snapshot with its quiet trees "frozen" and its autumn sounds hushed. "This man measured his eagle and weighed it. He found out what food it liked best, how much sleep it needed, and how long its talons were. But only after he'd set it free and watched it soar high in the sunshine did he know much about an eagle."

So it is with the autumn season. It has many aspects. Colorful photographs show some of them. So do the paintings at a little art shop along the roadside. So do fall-foliage tours over Vermont roads.

But to know it fully, you must meet it on its own terms. Get out of your car and take a stroll. Sniff the breeze and feel the air. Listen. Lie on your back in a meadow. Maybe you'll hear the geese headed south, too. Or pause in a wooded clearing, listening to an unseen creature rustling in the leaves or to the brave piping of a single spring peeper who mixed up his months.

At dusk your heart may skip a beat as you hear a series of hoots far off in the woods. Chances are it's an owl. But it *could* be a bear; after all, there's a bear for every square mile-and-a-half of the Green Mountain forest, and they hoot often in the fall.

It's things like these that give full dimension to the season—when you let all your senses tell you that it's autumn in Vermont.

The Absent-minded Hoarder

RONALD ROOD: *On Squirrels*

ROBERT CANDY Illustrations

IT'S NO WONDER THE WOODS ARE full of them. They have almost everything in their favor.

"They" are Vermont's five members of the squirrel family: red squirrel, gray squirrel, flying squirrel, chipmunk—and, surprisingly—the pudgy woodchuck, which is actually an outsized ground squirrel. Black squirrels, so common in New York State and Ontario, are seldom seen in Vermont. They are really only a color phase of the gray, and are sometimes found in the same litter.

Look at a squirrel and you will readily see how everything fits. Every boy who has ever tossed a dart or shot an arrow can guess how handy that feathery tail must be as a flight stabilizer. And anyone who has ever tried to lift a cat off the upholstery knows the value of sharp, curved claws for clinging.

That isn't all. Since a squirrel has to be on guard forever against enemies, its bulging eyes are far out on the sides of its head. Thus it can see forward, backward, up, down and sideways. However, even with panoramic vision, it may miss some vital detail of its surroundings. So nature has given it the ability to hustle food to a storehouse where it can consume it later.

It's this latter habit that often gets the squirrel in trouble. Nobody cares much if it squirrels away a quart or two of wild cherry pits. But if it starts in on the hickory nuts you've been waiting to harvest, that's another matter.

Actually, it's a good bet that the hickory tree is there in the first place because of the squirrel's great-great-grandparents. Although the soft-furred rodents are inveterate hoarders, they also tend to be hopelessly forgetful. They may bury a seed or a nut or an apple and never return. This no doubt accounts for a number of those wild apple trees growing in the middle of the woods, or a solitary butternut along a fencerow. They could well have been started by some absent-minded squirrel which carried the seed from place to place and finally deserted it.

Our own gray squirrel, Sparky, shows us just how strong this urge to hide things can be. Sparky was raised on a medicine dropper by the family of David Wroten in Burlington, and came to us when he was half grown. Now he enjoys the freedom of the big maples on our front lawn. When we call him down for his daily ration of sunflower seeds, he eats until he's full.

Then the fun begins. Taking a seed from my hand, he runs down to my trousers cuff. Poking the seed into the cuff, he returns for another. Or he may start in on my pockets. Or if I don't let him fill these, he tries to tuck seeds down my neck.

In a different way, many a roadside owes its great variety of edible plants to the squirrels. When one of these little creatures eats a raspberry or blackberry or highbush cranberry, the seeds pass through its intestines unharmed. Voided later as the animal runs along the fence that commonly parallels the road, the seeds are deposited—complete with a little pat of natural fertilizer—right where they'll sprout the first chance they get.

Of course birds and mice help in this natural gardening process, too. Biologists can often tell what food plants are common to an entire region just by the growth along the roadside.

Sparky's buck teeth make short work of almost anything he chews. He's forever nibbling, whether it's a nut or a seed or the garden hose as it lies on the lawn. Like most rodents, his urge to chew comes from more than a need to while away his time. His teeth are constantly growing: without something to wear them down, they would become so long as to be useless.

A friend of mine found a squirrel skull in Starksboro. One tooth had been broken away. Its mate in the other jaw, with nothing to wear against, had grown up and back in a semicircle, like the tusk of a wild boar. The unlucky squirrel had probably died of starvation.

Usually, however, starvation is no worry. Every tree and shrub has fruit or seeds of some kind. Most of them are considered fair game for a squirrel—with a little variety added in the form of an occasional insect or a few mushrooms.

Such a diet is fine for the gray squirrel. It usually suffices for our seldom-seen, nocturnal flying squirrel, too. Chipmunks and red squirrels, though, may stray further from a vegetarian diet. A striped chipmunk poking in the leaves comes across all kinds of edibles—snails, insects, earthworms. But red squirrels, sometimes tiring of the habit of sitting on a stump and peeling the scales off innumerable pine cones for the seeds, may go searching on far less commendable errands.

The underhanded activities of these rust-colored rodents came to me full force last spring. We had been happily watching the home-building of a pair of bluebirds in a nest box at the edge of our lawn. One day both parents were flying about in front of the box, chirping as if something was wrong. So I went to the box and tapped on the side.

At once there was a loud scolding from within the nest. Then the head of a red squirrel poked out. Before I'd decided how to capture him, he made a flying leap to freedom. When I opened the box, three of the four blue eggs had been crushed and the contents eaten. Although the fourth was intact, the bluebirds never came back. Luckily, however, a bird disturbed before the eggs hatch will usually build another nest in a new spot. So what might have been a tragedy was probably just a misfortune.

When it comes to their own nests, the members of the squirrel family are individualists. Although chipmunks are quite at home in trees, they have their nests underground. Lined with leaves and grass, they're built in a hidden chamber well below the surface. Thus the striped little fellows show their kinship to the ground squirrels of the West, and even the prairie dogs and woodchucks—which in reality are large squirrels.

To find the nest of a flying squirrel, rap on a decayed tree which has a few old woodpecker holes in a dead stub. If you're lucky, two or three gray-brown heads will

146

Clockwise: flying squirrel, woodchuck, and chipmunk.

poke out of a hole. The huge, liquid-dark eyes will tell you that you're in the presence of one of America's most appealing rodents—the soft-furred nocturnal creature with a flap of skin on either side from wrist to ankle. With these flaps, when it spreads its legs, it makes itself into a sailplane able to glide as much as one hundred feet if it starts high enough.

A pair of gray squirrels may make a home in a hollow tree. Most often they line the hole with leaves, twigs and grass, but not always. Two years ago I was startled to see a great crumpled piece of newspaper go bounding up the side of an elm in Middlebury. It was spirited aloft by a gray squirrel, which poked the day's news into a hole. The noisy process took several minutes, during which the squirrel almost fell when it tried to cling to the newspaper and push it in at the same time.

Red squirrels, always odd-man-out, often take whatever nest is handy—even if the rightful owner is still in residence. If it

147

happens to be the home of a thrush or tanager, the squirrel may consume the eggs. Then it casually roofs the home over with leaves right in the face of the outraged residents. And even though it's smaller than the gray squirrel, it will quickly rout its larger cousin as well. Whenever they meet, the peaceable gray quits the scene in favor of its peppery red relative.

With the nest of a crow or hawk, however, the little chickaree (as the red squirrel is often called) prudently waits until it's sure the home is empty. Or it may move into a hollow tree—a one-way trip for even this sharp-toothed little imp if the hole happens to be inhabited by an owl.

New families often get a whirlwind start in the squirrel set. The practice of watching a pair of courting squirrels is not recommended for the weak of heart. They carry on their romance at top speed. Running out to the end of a limb, leaping fearlessly into space and barely catching themselves by clutching the leaves of a neighboring tree, they undergo twenty lovers' leaps a minute.

The female looks as if she were trying desperately to get away. Once in Burlington I saw a lovelorn pair of grays race full into the stream of traffic. The female made it in one dash across the street between cars, but the male was not so lucky. I caught my breath as he rushed wildly beneath one wheel of a station wagon and checked himself just short of being crushed by the other one. Then, after a hasty glance to get his bearings, he continued the chase.

His lady, of course, had waited for him. Now she began anew her frantic efforts to escape.

In contrast to the somewhat debonair attitude on the part of the male, the female makes a faultless parent. Even the little red chickaree, so careless about the rights of other families, will chatter and scold and even attack if an enemy comes too close. Such parental concern is necessary, for the young, born about five weeks after mating, are completely helpless.

We were given a pair of baby chipmunks last May. They were the survivors of four youngsters which had been orphaned by a cat. Naked and blind, they were little more than animated appetites. We fed them sweetened milk with a medicine dropper until they were old enough to go out in July, find their own seeds, nibble their own flower heads, and punch their holes in our lawn.

In the process of raising a family, the female may yield to the homemaker's universal impulse. She is seized with the urge to rearrange the furniture. This may involve merely relining the nest, or it may mean moving to an entirely new location. If it's the latter, the babies must be carried to the second home. I've been privileged to see the process in woodchucks, chipmunks, reds and grays. The nocturnal flying squirrel does her moving at night. The babies are gently grasped by the belly in such a way that they can curl up and cling to both sides of the mother's face. Hanging thus upside down, the little fur collars make the trek to their new home.

Baby squirrels have to learn to climb. Their little claws are sharp from birth, but a squirrel on its own for the first time seems scared to death. It plasters itself against the trunk, moving with such caution that it looks as if it would never make it. But the playfulness which is part of all squirrels soon asserts itself. Then the hesitant crawl develops into the bouncing exuberance which leaves you breathless as you watch.

It's not true that a squirrel never falls. Our little chipmunks got into a fight in the top of a maple tree not long ago. Chattering and scolding, they forgot themselves. One lost his footing and fell nearly forty

Gray squirrel

149

Red squirrel

feet to the lawn. Shaking himself, he rushed right back up for Round Two. And Sparky, our gray squirrel, has tumbled to earth several times.

Finally, as summer wears on, squirrel youngsters go their own ways. A nest of flying squirrels which had entertained us all one spring with squeakings and caterwaulings in our attic was silent by August. A red squirrel family in our spruce grove got along fine together until September, when a whopping domestic quarrel sent them all packing in different directions.

From then until winter, the chief business seems to be to tuck away as much food as possible. The woodchuck, of course, stores it as a layer of fat for his winter sleep. Chipmunks, also great sleepers, fill their cheek pouches time and again with seeds or grain, and build up underground storehouses. Then they may curl up in the middle of their treasure and fall asleep.

For the true tree squirrels, however, winter is just another season. The gray squirrel in its elm or hardwoods, the red in its hemlocks and coniferous forests, and the flying squirrel in its old stub in the forest merely fall back on the seeds and nuts they've been gathering on their acre of land all autumn. If a squirrel has been industrious—and another squirrel hasn't pilfered its provisions—it may actually grow fat in winter. Besides, when the pantry's empty, the nearest tree has more buds and twigs. And with about two-thirds of Vermont covered by forest, that's a lot of buds.

So it's no wonder the woods are full of them.

"Chickaree"   BULLATY-LOMEO

151

BUTTERNUT

AMERICAN CHESTNUT

SHAGBARK
HICKORY

RED OAK

Woodland Harvest

EDWARD J. BRUNDAGE

Nature's yield in the autumn season, when it comes to nuts, finds its way for the most part to Vermont's denizens of the woods and fields. The humans, perversely, choose the scarce and hard-to-crack butternut and, so doing, compete only with the squirrel. Humans like them in maple sugar, while the squirrel takes them plain, eaten from his winter storehouse, or from the human's if he can pilfer from it.

The beechnut, which is common over most of Vermont, in good years furnishes much of the autumn and early winter mast for the black bear. His claw marks leave telltale black scars on the silver-gray bark.

The deer, the ruffed grouse and even the blue jay wax plump on the beechnuts. The jay is partial, also, to the acorns, as are the wild ducks. Chipmunks and raccoons have more catholic tastes when it comes to nuts, often eating from the shagbark hickory's fruits and the hazel nuts.

BLACK
WALNUT

AMERICAN
HAZEL

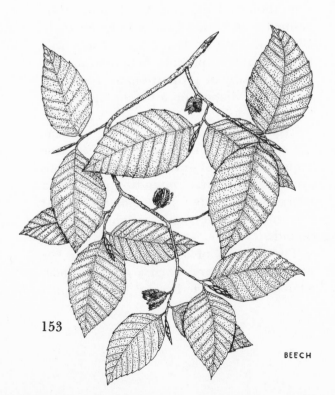

153

BEECH

The Black Bear

RONALD ROOD

ROBERT CANDY Illustration

IF ALL THE ODDS WERE IN YOUR favor, and you were able to travel without scent or sound, you could see a black bear in every one and a half square miles of the Green Mountain National Forest. Theoretically that's how common *Ursus americanus* is in Vermont, and means that here bears are crowded together about as closely as in any national forest in the United States.

However, many an old-timer has lived all his life in Vermont and has yet to see his first bear. The ears and nose of the big, thick-furred creature seldom allow it to be caught unawares. And in spite of its bulk, it can make its way through the woods with barely a sound.

It can "freeze" like a rabbit when necessary. The first black bear I ever saw in the wild ran across the road in front of the car. My friend slammed on the brakes and I jumped out with the camera, hoping to get a picture. But from the sounds of crashing brush, we knew we'd never see it again. We stood talking for a few moments, examining the tracks in the dust. Then we got back into the car.

When my friend touched the starter, the bushes at our right seemed to explode. A second bear, not twenty feet from us, had been quietly taking it all in until the sound of the motor startled it. Now it, too,

bounded away, leaving me with a blurred snapshot and a tingling spine.

Woodsmen tell me that one rarely sees two adult bears together like that, especially in early June. Also, the bear is usually so timid that it flees headlong, rather than hiding quietly. In spite of its strength, its full array of teeth, and its sharp curving claws, it would rather run than fight.

Our largest Eastern carnivore starts life modestly. The drowsy mother has her two or three cubs in January in her den beneath the roots of an old tree or in a sheltered cave. They are tiny in proportion to their two-hundred-pound mother—how tiny, though, I did not realize until I examined a specimen from a museum shelf. Weighing less than ten ounces, it was little larger than a chipmunk. A human mother having a baby of proportionate size would be pinning diapers on a tot no larger than her fist.

Even at five weeks, when their eyes begin to open and their naked bodies have acquired a coat of gray hair, the little cubs average only three pounds apiece. And when they're ready for their first outing at two months, they still weigh only five pounds.

The concern of a mother bear for her babies is legendary. Even a grumpy male, who may outweigh her by half as much

154

again, is careful not to separate the family. She flies at him like a spitfire. But if she keeps at it, he feels called on to assert his authority, and may soundly thrash her before he leaves the scene. Even then, she turns first to her babies before licking her own wounds.

No adult males are allowed in the family group, Goldilocks to the contrary. The cubs may stay with their mother for as long as a year and a half, sharing sleeping quarters for the first winter. By then, they may weigh fifty pounds or more. It's lucky that the female has babies only every other year,

as brand-new little fellows would come out second best if they were born in the den with big sprawling brothers or sisters.

When the she-bear finally relents of her matriarchy and answers the call to romance in late June or July, she turns her back on her half-grown offspring of the year before. Pairing off with a male, she travels with him for a few days or weeks.

The deserted cubs soon part company. They become wanderers for the rest of their lives, starting on new families of their own at three and a half years. Their first-born come about seven months later, when

155

they are about four years old.

Almost any wooded area, sufficiently wild and sufficiently big, will suit them. In fact, the black bear has been seen, at one time or another, in practically every state of the Union, of course including Alaska, and in Mexico and all the Canadian provinces. Thus it is one of North America's widest-ranging creatures.

One afternoon I met a hiker at Battell Shelter on the Long Trail to Mt. Abraham. He told me a story which shows the bear's natural curiosity, timid though it may be.

After making camp along the trail the night before, the hiker had begun to hear stealthy sounds beyond the gleam of his fire. He shouted and tossed a stick in the direction of the sound. "Mice," he tried to convince himself.

All night he lay listening to the "mice." When dawn finally came, he went out to have a look. He found that a bear had apparently circled his camp several times.

"I've always wanted to see a bear," he told me, "but I was glad I didn't see that one—not in the middle of the night, at least."

Although bears will run from humans unless attacked, wounded or in defense of cubs, their curiosity got on the nerves of campers in the Adirondacks a few years ago. So conservationists figured this was a good time to catch, study, and relocate them. They made a trap consisting of a section of culvert, closed at one end and baited with a slab of bacon. When the bear entered and pulled at the bacon, it tripped a lever and a trap door fell down over the opening. Feeling the door slam on its hind quarters, the bear would jump farther into the culvert, there to remain until its captors arrived.

Etherized, tagged and weighed, they were released several miles from the camps they had disturbed. But they had a definite lik-

ing for the general locality. They had to be taken as much as twenty miles away to make sure they wouldn't return. One undaunted male found his way back to the same trap from a distance of forty-three miles.

Nobody knows for sure how large the black bear can grow. One New York specimen weighed six hundred five pounds. Vermont individuals of five hundred pounds are sometimes taken among the two hundred fifty or so killed each year from September 1 to the end of November. But it's hard to get exact sizes because they are usually killed and field-dressed miles from the nearest scales.

One black bear in a zoo lived twenty-four years, but it's doubtful that they last that long in the wild. Although they have no effective natural enemies, they face constant pressure from man and dogs. A craving for honey, plus killing an occasional lamb, colt, pig or calf may put a quick end to Bruin's career before he reaches full maturity at eight or ten years.

Searching through the files of the American Museum of Natural History for information, I asked one of the mammalogists for his impression of this creature's food habits.

A black bear, he told me, will eat anything a man will eat—and more besides. It has the digestion of a cement mixer. It's about seventy-five percent vegetarian, and will take skunk cabbage, bitter cherries, and even poison ivy leaves along with more tasty bits like nuts, acorns and fruit. But it likes insects, too. Sometimes it tears a hornets' nest to pieces for the grubs; those hornets will attack anything that comes near for several days afterward.

"Bears are flesh-eaters, too," he continued. "They rarely bother domestic animals, but go after mice, squirrels and chipmunks. They'll dig away a ton of dirt just to get at a mouse nest."

The big, ambling creature is well known for its sweet tooth. Poking around in the dump behind a woodland cabin, it discovers a jelly jar. Sitting down like a boy with a candy bar, it holds the jar in its paws and scours it out with its long tongue.

"Musquaw," as some Indians called it, was also known as the "animal that walks like a man." This was because of its flat-footed gait and its habit of standing erect to investigate a suspicious sound. Near-sighted, it samples the air with nose and ears before turning to flee.

It is fond of playing pranks, too. A friend of mine who keeps bees lost several hives to a honey-loving bear not many years ago. But his loss was small compared to that of a telephone company in New Hampshire. Bears tore or damaged about fifty poles—apparently under the impression that the humming of the wires was the sound of bees inside the "trees."

A summer camper found two rolls of roofing paper unrolled completely by a bear who must have been disappointed when the game—and the roofing—came to an end. Another camper watched a bear thrash the life out of a witch-hazel bush and walk away as if it had vanquished a mortal enemy.

Bruin may sit for half an hour, contemplating a stream of red ants crossing the trail. But when he wants to, he can be amazingly agile. He can shinny up a tree—and frequently does—or run as fast as any creature in the woods at an estimated thirty-five or forty miles per hour. Loving to swim, he's been seen paddling across Lake Champlain. His voice ranges from a whimper through a succession of woofs, grunts and snorts. When wounded, he may utter a startling cry that sounds human. Angered, he can voice a full-throated roar.

A roaming bear stops here and there to scratch a tree as high as it can reach; a sign-post, perhaps, for others of its kind. By fall, it has garnered layers of fat against the winter ahead. Finding a cozy den, it curls up before the snow is deep. But its sleep is light. The sound of a voice or the touch of a hand may rouse it. More than one startled person has discovered this when he poked it with a stick.

Such light slumber has led many scientists to feel that true hibernation—where the heartbeat slows almost to a stop and breathing approaches zero—is something for bats and woodchucks and not for the black bear.

When spring comes north again, the bears cease living on capital and start living on income. They poke around for acorns, beechnuts, Jack-in-the-pulpit roots, and early insects. The constant demands of the cubs sometimes wear their mother's patience thin. Tiring of their complaints, she chases them up into a tree to baby-sit each other while she has a nap.

A forester told me recently of a mother with two cubs which he had watched through binoculars. "She left the cubs up on an old stump," he recalled, "and lay down beside it to sleep. But in a few minutes one of them crept down. She chased him up again.

"Would he take 'no' for an answer? Of course not. He sneaked down on the back side so she wouldn't see him. But she caught him just the same and whacked him so hard he howled. Then she cuffed him all the way back to the top.

"All this time his good-goody brother was sitting up there, smug as a cat. I could almost see a smile on his face.

"Well, when little Junior got there the last time, he sidled up to his brother. Then he looked down at his mother. She was sound asleep. So, with a roundhouse left, he knocked his brother flat."

Bats and Caves

HAROLD B. HITCHCOCK

THOUGH MANY PEOPLE SHRINK from entering caves because of the bats that inhabit them in season, it is the bats that for the past twenty-five years have been luring me into Vermont caves. My interest in studying the distribution of the various species of bats in the state, their sex ratios and migrations, has made me a cave explorer.

Bats use caves mostly in the winter, when they require a protected place to hibernate. Since the bat lives entirely on flying insects, little food is available from about the middle of September until April. Like the better-known woodchuck, the bat puts on fat during the summer, then by letting its temperature drop to that of the surrounding cave until spring, uses the fat up slowly.

Vermont's commonest bat is the little brown bat, *Myotis l. lucifugus*. For hibernation, its preference is for a temperature in the low forties or upper thirties, and it will hang up in caves, usually in clusters, where the temperature is right. As the cave becomes cooler with the advance of winter, bats shift from the more exposed to better sheltered areas within it. Moisture-laden air moving into the cave may cover some bats with droplets of dew, until each hair is tipped with a glistening jewel. At a distance the bat may appear white. If someone tells you about albino bats seen in a cave, you can be pretty sure they were really only dew-covered.

Bats wake up and fly around from time to time during the winter, even in parts of the cave where temperature conditions are optimum. Aroused from deep hibernation, a bat requires fifteen or twenty minutes to become active enough to fly.

In the spring the females leave the cave before the males. They have already mated, and need to get their young born early enough in the summer for them to be able to get fattened up for the hibernation to come. The sociable females make themselves unpopular in the summertime with many a Vermonter by their choice of roosts in attics and other dark, warm retreats in buildings. In these colonies, which may have from a dozen or so bats up to several hundred, the young are born. No nests are built, and the single baby that is customarily born about the middle of June may cling to its mother as she leaves the roost for food at dusk. Growth is rapid, and after a day or two the baby is left behind in the attic while the mother seeks food and water.

During the summer adult males are rarely encountered inside buildings. Possibly they find the maternity centers too crowded, hot and smelly. At any rate, they stay outside, hiding during the daytime beneath loose bark, behind shutters, and in other retreats.

A few bats may be found in caves weeks before frost. These are probably transients; possibly they are testing for a suitable place in which to hibernate. Banding has shown that bats return faithfully year after year to the same cave, just as the females do to their summer roosts. The distance between the summer and winter homes of the little

brown bat may be as great as one hundred and sixty-five miles.

Studies in progress at this writing, 1962, show that in the spring bats using the cave on Mount Aeolus near East Dorset (shown in John F. Smith's photograph) scatter conspicuously to the southeast, across southern New Hampshire to eastern Massachusetts and Rhode Island. Some, of course, remain close by, but we know that bats may pass up caves near their summer range and hibernate at a distance.

Recent publicity about a bat cave in Texas and the menace of bat-borne rabies has alerted the public to the danger of exposure to bats. The little brown bat and other species that occur in Vermont have been implicated as carriers of rabies. For that reason one should not handle bats; professional bat workers get immunizing injections to protect them. Because bats are valuable as insect destroyers, they should not be molested except where they are a nuisance in buildings.

One need have no fear, however, of Vermont caves, themselves, for they are totally unlike the bat caves in the Southwest, where, it has been reported, the very air may carry the rabies virus.

Most of Vermont's caves occur in limestone and marble formations in the western part of the state. They were formed by the dissolution of the rock by water, and streams still flow in some, though more often no stream is found. Water that drips from the ceilings collects at the bottom of the cave or seeps through the floor.

Possibly because of the area's glacial history, Vermont caves are not as large as American caves go. A few hundred feet in length is as big as you'll find. And many of the passageways are not designed for walking. Crawling or slithering is the means of locomotion. Because of their limited size you don't need to worry about getting lost in them. The better-known caves are also relatively safe with respect to the stability of their walls and ceilings. Greater danger lies underfoot where slippery rocks invite falls. A safety hat is appropriate even if it is more to protect the wearer from crashing his head against the roof than from falling rock.

Vermont caves lack the spectacular formations characteristic of many commercialized caves. Flowstone on walls is about all one can point to; large stalactites have not formed, and the small ones originally present have, for the most part, been broken off by souvenir hunters.

Each winter, however, a beautiful crop of ice formations develops at the mouth of several of the caves. Those with small entrances, like Nickwackett (in Chittenden) and Plymouth, sport a delicate fringe of hoarfrost at the mouth. Warm moisture-laden air from the cave, striking the colder objects outside, drops its water as crystals on the rocks and nearby plants.

Within the caves, water dripping from the roof to the cold floor builds stalagmites;

as winter advances the roof of the cave may become cold enough for ice stalactites to form near the entrance. Sometimes the advancing formations meet, forming ice pillars and curtains. Seen with artificial light against the dark walls of the cave, these seasonal formations excel in beauty their stony counterparts. The larger ones may last into the summer, shrinking gradually as the season advances.

Back in 1936 when I began my cave-crawling, few people visited Vermont caves. However, the caves had been both known and visited for a long time, as ancient initials and dates carved in cave walls forcefully testify. But the earlier visits were largely impromptu, by local groups relying on candles and kerosene lanterns.

Today, though, cave exploration has become a sport; enthusiasts from New York and other cities spend Vermont weekends probing into even the remotest caves. College outing clubs run organized cave trips; summer camps do the same. Even the serious scientific visitors have increased, for bats have achieved popularity as research animals. Carbide and gasoline vapor lanterns and battery-powered lamps have replaced the candle and kerosene lantern.

Unfortunately the bats have not taken kindly to these intrusions. Where hundreds could be found in caves in 1936 only a handful can be found in the early 1960's.

The sports-minded cave crawler is known as a spelunker. He will not leave a cave until he has squirmed into every crawlway that his body can possibly be squeezed through. You encounter him mostly during the non-skiing months, but long before the last snow has melted from the wooded slopes he's back again to initiate some newcomers or to get to the end of the passage he's heard about but "must have overlooked" on the last trip.

For the benefit of such cave detectives, I

offer the following account. It is from *Geography Made Easy,* by Jedidiah Morse, D.D., and published in 1819. Even back then this book was in its twentieth edition.

"In the town of Clarendon, on the side of a small hill, is a very curious cave. The chasm, at its entrance, is about 4 feet in circumference. Entering this, you descend 104 feet, and then opens a spacious room 20 feet in breadth, and 100 feet in length; the roof of this cavern is of rock, through which the water is continually percolating. The stalactites which hang from the roof appear like icicles on the eaves of houses, and are continually increasing in number and magnitude.

"The bottom and sides are daily incrusting with spar and other mineral substances. On the sides of this subterraneous hall are tables, chairs, etc. which appear to have been artificially carved. This richly ornamented room, when illuminated with the candles of the guides, has an enchanting effect upon the eye of the spectator. At the end of the cave is a circular hole, 15 feet deep, apparently hewn out, in a conical form, enlarging gradually as you descend, in the form of a sugar loaf. At the bottom is a spring of fresh water, in continual motion, like the boiling of a pot. It's depth has never been sounded."

I'd like to see this cave, and I have tried to find it. Roy Webster, superintendent of the Vermont Marble Company's Danby quarry, guided me to a cave in the area, Colvin's Cave. It is on a hillside (which is very likely to be the case anywhere in Clarendon), its entrance is about four feet in diameter, and at the end is a pool of water.

But the pool was not boiling when I saw it; and its depth was scarcely four feet. Between the entrance and the pool, little corresponded to the Reverend Mr. Morse's

description. Could it be that under the enchanting influence of the guides' candles, things looked different to him? Or might it even be that the good geographer never visited the cave, but accepted at face value the tall tales of others?

There is another cave that perhaps needs further exploration—the one on Mount Aeolus, referred to earlier. In the *Geology of Vermont* (1861), Professor Edward Hitchcock notes that the cave was "obviously" formed by an ancient river. Although unable himself to penetrate very far, he reasoned that the cave must continue, probably passing right through the mountain. Lest his reader be in doubt as to his meaning, he even drew a diagram showing an opening on the opposite side.

One could start looking for the missing part at either end, I suppose. If able to confirm the professor's hypothesis, one would really have found a cave that should be described in the next edition of Morse's *Geography Made Easy* (which by now must be in at least the fiftieth edition).

Some caves have a way of disappearing entirely. You'll encounter the old hunter who came across a cave years ago and has never been able to find it again, "and it was a real big one at that." Dimensions of other caves reported to you, the number of bats within them, may tend toward the sensational: the caves, for example, which "go clean through the mountain" and have bats so numerous "you have to keep ducking to keep them from flying into your face."

If you want to explore for caves, the marble and limestone belt should keep you busy a good while. In other parts of the state, talus and fault caves can be found. To get leads, inquire of local inhabitants or look up "Underground Vermont," in the Spring 1956 issue of *Vermont Life,* and also *Caves of Vermont,* by John Scott.

161

November

SONJA BULLATY and
ANGELO LOMEO:

An Essay in Black and White

Not yesterday I learned to know
   The love of bare November days
Before the coming of the snow

ROBERT FROST

162

The Crow

RONALD ROOD

ROBERT CANDY Illustrations

SOME TIME AGO A GROUP OF wildlife experts got together. In keeping with the spirit of the times, perhaps, they decided that the common crow must be investigated. So they banded hundreds of the big black birds, quizzed hikers and fishermen, and solemnly peered into some two thousand crow stomachs.

Eventually when they'd collected a roomful of data, they released their report: the crow ate at least six hundred and fifty different kinds of food and was found over nearly all of our continent from Alaska to Newfoundland to Mexico.

At this, one long-suffering, taxpaying farmer exploded. "Heck," he sputtered, "why'd they go to all that trouble? Anybody knows that crows are everywhere and eat everything!"

He was pretty close to the truth, even to the "anybody knows" part. There's an old saying that if a person can recognize only three birds, one of them will be a crow. And that same person is also likely to know lots about the crow's life story—most of it bad.

With six hundred and fifty items of food in its diet, however, it can't all be bad. Actually, you can search through the list and find plenty of evidence to support any stand—pro-crow or anti-crow—you wish to take.

As an example, the crow makes short work of baby snapping turtles as they hatch from their eggs near Lake Champlain. This, of course, delights the duck hunter who has long claimed that snappers destroy thousands of duckling annually. On the other hand, if there are no baby turtles handy, the crow is happily impartial. It starts in on the duckling itself.

You don't necessarily have to search through a crow's innards to get your information, though. Just watch a flock of them as they follow a farmer and his plow. They're busy pecking at the newly turned soil, eating quantities of grubs and insects. I pointed this out to a neighbor one day as we watched the crows in the far corner of his field.

His reaction was quick and positive. "And do you know *why* they're eating the bugs?" he countered. "So they'll have the corn all to themselves."

Although the crow doesn't really have that much intelligence, sometimes it almost seems that it has. It hasn't been called a "feathered Ph.D." for nothing. Its actions may border so closely on rationality that it's difficult to remember it's only a bird.

A crow can spot the difference between a man with a stick and a man with a gun, for instance. While it's true that the hunter behaves differently from the hiker, few other creatures make any distinction. They just run from all humans to be safe. And while you may surprise almost any other animal while it is feeding, you'll seldom get that chance with a crow. In the first place, it rarely travels alone. Then, too, it almost always keeps a sentinel posted for danger.

One measure of quick-wittedness is the ability of any creature—from man on down—to size up a new situation. An ornithologist told me of a pet crow which was fed some stale crusts of bread. The food was so hard that the bird had trouble eating it. But this didn't bother it one bit. It merely took the bread over to its dish of drinking water. There it swizzled it around until it was just the right softness. Then it bolted it down without ruffling a feather.

Another pet crow, like its cousins the jays, magpies and ravens, was fond of bright objects. It was a confirmed kleptomaniac. It stole bits of tinfoil, buttons, even eyeglasses and jewelry when it had the chance. One day a man offered it a pocket knife. When the crow pecked at the shiny instrument, the man snatched it away. Several times this tantalizing process was repeated.

Finally, when the knife was offered once more, the crow pecked the man's hand instead. The man dropped the knife in surprise—and the crow snatched it up. Then it triumphantly bore its trophy to the top of a dead tree. It had persisted until it got the desired result. Probably this doesn't show any real intelligence on the part of the crow, which may have pecked just in anger. But then, it doesn't show much intelligence on the part of the man, either.

I've seen a wild crow play a game similar

to Button-Button, too. As we used to play the game the person who knew where the button was hidden would say "warmer" or "colder" according to the movements of the one searching for it. This was the way it happened to a crow in a field in Swanton two years ago as I watched it from a distance with binoculars.

The crow landed in some newly cut hay, looking for insects. Its random wanderings brought it to the vicinity of a red-winged blackbird's nest at the edge of the field. The red-wing began to chirp and flit nervously.

The crow, sensing bigger prey, forgot its search for grasshoppers and began to walk in different directions. As it drew near to the nest, the blackbird's cries increased; when it walked in the wrong direction the smaller bird relaxed.

Thus guided, it finally "homed in" on the nest. When I finally got to the scene of the tragedy later, I found the nest destroyed. But luckily it had contained only eggs and no young, so the blackbirds undoubtedly were able to start a new family elsewhere.

Clever as a crow may be most of the year, though, it seems to forget itself at mating time. A pair of crows in the spring may be as silly as lambs. Most of the antics are put on by the male, but his intended partner joins in when she feels like it. They swoop low and zoom high, sometimes turning somersaults in the air. Possibly as a term of endearment either crow may utter what one book calls "the love song." To my ears, however, it sounds more like a dog crunching a bone.

The aerobatics completed, the two may bill and caress each other like doves on a branch, or they may flee from one tree to another, the female pursued by the male but somehow never quite seeming to be able to escape.

This isn't always done just in pairs. Sometimes several may get the fever at once. A small flock of gamboling crows looks from a distance like wind-tossed leaves.

How to tell male from female apparently is clear to the crows, but even a crow can make a mistake. Sometimes a male will chase another male until the outraged recipient of this attention puts things straight in no uncertain terms.

At other times four or five males will chase a single female while other females are neglected. "But," sighed a lady ornithologist who told me about this, "I guess that's life."

Nesting begins in April. The nest is a bulky affair of twigs and sticks, usually well hidden in the top of a tall evergreen. Although it looks crude, a crow's nest is actually well built and may last for years. It's deep and cuplike within, lined with hair, soft shreds of bark or bits of fur. It has the capacity of a mixing bowl to accommodate the female or her slightly larger mate, whose length may exceed twenty inches.

Since there's sometimes a scarcity of tall evergreens, other trees may have to be used, or several crows may nest in the same tree. Then, too, three crows have been known to share the same nest. A book on birds, in commenting on this scandalous state of affairs, managed to keep a strictly scientific approach to the eternal triangle. "Since the sexes are so similar," it reported, "it is impossible to tell whether polygamy or

polyandry is being practiced."

Raucous crows are silent crows near the nest. They fly to their home by a devious route. Then they steal quietly to the nest and settle down like shadows. The last crow's nest I inspected was typical. It had four greenish eggs a little smaller than ping-pong balls, spotted with brown.

The eggs hatch in about eighteen days. Baby crows are naked and blind at first, are silent and helpless, but in less than a week their eyes are open. From hatching until they fly away more than a month later, their main interest in life is food. They may easily consume half their weight in food every day. So my four crow's eggs, if they produced normal, one-pound birds, represented half a hundred pounds of food that would be flown up to that tree by the parents.

This food probably was made up of everything from eggs and nestlings of other birds to fruit, insects, and even carrion. In fact, Vermont crows do the same job as vultures in the South, cleaning up car-killed animals on the highway.

Parental silence is quickly made up for by the cries of the youngsters. You can hear a nest of baby crows half a mile away when the wind is right. If the call of the adults can be described as "caw, caw," the young would be characterized as "car, car." It's at this noisy stage that the young are usually taken by enterprising schoolboys who gather them at considerable personal risk. It's no small task to fight off a pair of determined adults, cling to a swaying treetop and capture an active youngster.

It's surprising how many ways a crow can say "caw." It plays almost endless variations on this single theme—a short, quick danger call, a longer rallying call, a food call, and a "mob" call, used when it spies a hawk or owl, which is pestered until it flies away.

The crow is a wonderful mimic, too. A few years ago we had a little puppy tied to a tree in the back yard. He yelped and wailed as if he was about to catch pneumonia in the September sun. Then suddenly his cries increased in volume.

"Maybe we'd better go see if he's all right," my wife said. There sat our puppy, wailing piteously, while above him were three crows. Every time he'd yelp, they'd yelp right back. And it was hard to tell which cry was the most agonizing.

Pet crows are as good at mimicking as their wild brothers. (And you do *not* have to split their tongues to help them talk. That old belief is cruel and senseless.) One of my boyhood chums had a crow which could laugh or cry. It even got so that it could say "hello" and "howdy-do" and "goodbye."

It also learned to swear, a trick picked up all by itself. Swear words usually are uttered loudly, distinctly and emphatically —and it didn't take Inky long to get the hang of them. Of course none of us boys ever had any idea where it heard such words.

Wild or tame, *Corvus brachyrhynchos* (meaning "the crow with the short beak") is fully grown by early fall. Now the families gather together in small groups. These in turn congregate in larger groups and finally into huge flocks. It's these flocks that so effectively can mob the great horned owl. This predator is about the only one which the crow has good reason to fear, for the owl can easily nab a crow while it's sleeping. So great is the enmity between the two that hunters often mount a stuffed

170

owl in a tree. Then they sit back to wait for the fun.

As autumn advances, the great flocks leave such places as my Lincoln hills and head for the milder lowlands. I don't see them again until March. Corn left standing in the field on the flat farms near Lake Champlain may feed them all winter. Other flocks winter along the lake itself, or even migrate to the seashore, where they forage along the beach by day, feeding on anything the tide brings up. If a shell is too hard, a crow may fly above a rock and drop it until it breaks.

At night they sleep in great rookeries, coming from all points of the compass to a chosen grove of trees. They fill the air with commotion as they flap and caw and hop from branch to branch.

Occasionally such rookeries are the ob-

jects of concerted attacks by irate farmers and sportsmen who figure that the only good crow is a dead one. Planting dynamite bombs in the ground beneath the trees, they blow thousands of the birds to kingdom come each year.

One sportsmen's group noted that a huge flock of these birds was roosting in a clump of trees near a lake. Night after night the crows came by the thousands. So the men spent part of one day and all of the next wiring the trees and concealing lethal charges of dynamite along the limbs at strategic points.

After all was in readiness, the men gathered in a little knot to witness the destruction that would take place when they pushed the fatal plunger.

And you guessed it. Not a single crow showed up.

171

White-Tail

RONALD ROOD: *On the Deer*

EDWARD J. BRUNDAGE Illustration

IF YOU'VE EVER STARTLED A white-tailed deer, you know how it got its name. That nine-inch tail, snow white on the underside, flips up like a flag. Then it wags back and forth with each bound of the retreating animal.

Vermont's most common large wild animal gets its start in a thicket in late May or June. The tiny fawns, weighing as little as three and one half, or as much as seven pounds, arrive with their eyes fully open. A first-time mother usually has just a single baby, but twins are common thereafter. Occasionally there are triplets. Floppier even than a newborn calf, the little fawn can hardly stand alone. It lies stretched out on its stomach, the white spots on its rusty coat matching the dappled undergrowth.

Next, the little fellow gets scrubbed. His mother's rough, long tongue goes all over his soft hair coat. Once this was thought to be just a brisk rub-down. However, it has another value too. Once she has licked him and breathed on him, the doe will know her baby from then on.

This is important, especially if he's one of twins. Each twin is left by the mother in a different place. Thus she spreads the risk. Nursing each within a short time after birth, she then steals away to feed on twigs and weeds. She comes back only to nurse, thus not betraying the secret hiding-places by her presence at other times.

It's while the mother is away that most "lost" fawns are found by hikers or vacationists. Of course, the little fellow is no more lost than if he were a bird in a nest. The best thing is to let him be. Chances are that his mother is somewhere within a few hundred yards.

Naturalists say the fawn has no scent. A bear or dog may pass harmlessly within inches of it. To give further protection, a doe surprised near her baby may dash off noisily, uttering a barking "whoof" with every bound, thus calling attention to herself. Sometimes she may even stay and fight.

The mother feeds her fawns about five times daily. In between, the babies lie concealed in a little nest, or "form." Gradually, however, their curiosity prods them to action. Getting up on wobbly legs, they begin to sample twigs and leaves. They seldom wander far, and melt into the forest floor at any strange noise.

Then one day the spotted fawn asserts himself. Before, he would allow himself to be pushed down to the ground by his mother's nose as she prepared to leave. Now that he's a month old, he'll have none of it. Trotting along after her, he goes with her on her feeding rounds. Then he may discover something he's suspected all along: there's another fawn just like him under a spruce a little way off.

He spends the rest of that summer with his mother, often remaining with her until next May's fawns are born. If they should become separated, he has several ways of finding her again. First, there's that waving white flag. Second, he (and she) can bleat like a lamb, calling until they are reunited. Third, she has little glands between her hoofs which scent her footprints and lead him "home." Other glands near her eyes have a faint ammonia smell which lingers briefly near the vegetation where she feeds. So a fawn can find his mother with eyes, ears and nose.

A fawn at my boyhood Scout camp was the official mascot one summer. Late in the season some of us went back to put away the floats and canoes. Rufus was still there, but he was rapidly growing up. Now some six months old, he weighed perhaps fifty pounds. His trusting ways had taken on a new aloofness. Little nubbins on his head showed where the antlers would be, although they wouldn't actually begin to grow until the following year.

The biggest change, however, was in his coat. Sometime between the closing of camp and this October afternoon, he had traded his dappled baby clothes for a new salt-and-pepper overcoat. Its grayishness, I learned later, was due largely to air cells within the hair itself. These would serve as winter insulation and as floats for swimming.

Deer are great swimmers. They can easily cross four or five miles of water, a stretch as wide as much of Lake Champlain. They are also fond of water plants. A woodland scene hard to forget is a buck and a doe I once saw at the edge of a lake. They were submerged almost to the shoulders, feeding on underwater vegetation like their huge cousin, the moose. In fact, the Indians used to call them "stream deer" because of their fondness for water.

Often the white-tail takes to the water for a different reason. When flies are thick, it finds a marsh, pond-edge or trout pool. Sinking until only its head shows, it relieves itself of their torment in the cool water. The size of a stream in which it can find rest is astonishing. It may lie down in one

so small that its body blocks it completely. Then the water rises, finally to flow over this living dam, effectively keeping the flies at a distance.

Only the very rare (and probably abnormal) female deer has any sign of antlers. However, the sharp, polished hoofs are dangerous weapons. Stabbing on the upstroke, slashing on the downstroke, they are unbelievably quick, faster than the eye can see, and packed with power that could easily disembowel a dog.

Do the oldest bucks have the largest antlers? This question is good for a half-hour at any hunting lodge or camp. It's hard to resolve to a Yes or No. The deer in his second year may be a spikehorn, pronghorn or six-pointer depending on the quality of the range. As nutrition plays a vital part, poor antler growth may indicate a buck on poor feed or in advanced years.

The buck drops his antlers in winter. His next pair is usually larger, but this increase does not take place forever. After approximately three and a half to five years of age, antler size may level off or actually decrease. Beyond this, "racks" may be abnormal, unbalanced, or of poor form.

If you look at the thickness of the antler

173

just above the swollen base, you can make an educated guess as to the quality of the animal's range during the past growing season. Generally, thickness is proportional to range quality. This only serves to emphasize the astonishingly close relationship between the deer and all phases of its surroundings—soils, minerals, and available food.

The antlers of the deer family are among the fastest-growing bones known. Moose, caribou, deer and elk all form new ones each spring. Covered with soft skin, well supplied with blood, they remain "in the velvet" from spring until autumn. Then their owner polishes them by rubbing against bushes and trees. At the same time, his swelling neck and aggressive mood indicate that mating is fast approaching.

Tame deer, normally well mannered, may suddenly turn on their human friends. Occasionally even a wild buck may attack a human being during the rutting season.

People who tramp the woods are often unaware of the number of deer that may be around them. Although the white flag is the traditional mark of the startled deer, many may just lie low until danger is past. Others just sneak away, tail tucked down out of sight.

Summer menus are no problem for the white-tail. I've often seen them at dusk along the edges of fields, grazing on weeds and clover. In all, more than six hundred foods have been listed, with maple, birch, apple and cherry preferred among woods.

The deer bites off the twigs with a twisting motion, thus producing a peculiarly frayed end. Mushrooms, wintergreen, lichens, ferns and even last year's antlers also provide good nibbling. However, it's a lucky deer that finds a set of antlers to chew on. Mice, rabbits and porcupines like calcium, too, and speedily reduce them to lacework.

Winter feeding is starkly different. In the depth of soft snow the slender-legged deer is in real trouble. Able to travel ten miles with ease on a summer night—although its normal range is a mile or less—it is greatly restricted in winter. It gravitates to the swamps, white cedar thickets, or slopes with a favorable exposure, there to mill around with others of its kind.

Soon the snow is packed into trails and "yards" in the areas affording adequate shelter. As browse and twigs get used up, the deer begin to stand on their hind legs to reach higher food. Soon a "browse line" develops, with every available twig broken off up to the highest level reached by the tallest deer.

In a severe winter, youngsters and does may lose out in this deadly competition.

The whole problem of maintaining deer in Vermont is a weighty one. There is slightly better than one white-tail for every two people—some quarter-million deer according to the 1966-67 estimate. This makes about as high a ratio as you'll find anywhere in their range, which is from southern Canadian provinces clear to Central America, excluding our arid Southwest. However, from all the heat and light generated over *Odocoileus virginianus*, a few facts have emerged:

1. In many cases, deer are far more plentiful today than in pioneer times. Over a hundred years ago they were extinct in southern New England and even in southern Vermont. Valued for their hides, meat and antlers, they could not keep pace with the pressure put on them.

2. The original unbroken forests didn't favor large deer populations, as forest-floor cover and food were sparse. The deer concentrated largely along woods edges and openings, their numbers kept within the

limits of the carrying capacity of the land. Now, with the large-scale abandonment and increase in cutover land, whole areas have suddenly become woods edges and openings.

3. Much of this land, ideal in summer, is unusable by deer in winter, because of lack of shelter and unfavorable exposure. So the deer concentrate in the smaller protected yard areas.

4. The wolf, cougar (or panther), coyote, and even the occasional lucky bobcat, are no longer effective natural means of controlling deer. So man has lifted the lid on the white-tail in several ways at once. In spite of extended hunting seasons, though, the state's deer herd is increasing almost twenty percent a year.

A three-hundred-pound buck, live weight, is a fine specimen. Occasional animals have run to four hundred pounds, or over, and some does weigh over two hundred. However, the more they're crowded or poorly fed the smaller the average specimen. A deer may live twelve years or more on good range, but disease and starvation may cut its life in half.

The farmer woefully surveys his ruined crops and wishes for fewer deer. The hunter puts up his gun at the end of the season and wishes for more. So do the hikers and vacationists.

The lumberman complains that his young trees are severely cut back by deer, except where saplings have grown up through brush piles and slash. Showing a preference for maple, ash and other timber trees, the deer leave behind beech, hop hornbeam and other less valuable species. This will seriously affect Vermont's forests and wood-using industries in the future.

Somewhere in the middle of it all, trying for a neat balance, is Vermont's Fish and Game Department. It has to deal with too many deer in one instance, too few in another.

In the fall of 1961, shortly after the regular hunting period, it permitted the first quick "antler-less deer season" in certain counties. This was an effort to curb the population explosion among the deer.

"Basically, our recommendations are two-fold: timber practices and herd management," said George W. Davis, formerly Vermont's Fish and Game Commissioner. "It's not fair to manage one and disregard the other. All uses of the land are important. They are interdependent. There's no other way around it."

The soft-eyed, large-eared, tawny-red (in summer) or gray (in winter) animal with the white bib and nose-band, is always a thrill to see. Its speed of twenty-five miles per hour, and its great leaps, sometimes exceeding twenty feet on the straightaway and eight feet into the air, make it a spectacular creature. In many parts of the state, "deer jams" occur. Cars line the road at dusk to watch the graceful creatures in the meadows.

The deer supplied man with his moccasins, jackets, blankets and knife-handles. On the frontier it has even provided fawn-skin underwear, greased hide windows and tallow candles. Its skin has been used for money, and helped open our country to explorers.

As America's most popular big-game animal, it supplies hunters with more than half a million trophies each year—some ten thousand of them from Vermont.

With such an illustrious history, there's small wonder that the white-tail was proposed as our state animal before the Morgan horse was officially so designated. Nevertheless, in the hearts of many who know it well, it still commands the same honored position it occupies on the State flag: topmost of all.

Victims of Slander

RONALD ROOD: *On Snakes*

ROBERT CANDY Illustrations

IT MUST BE HARD TO BE A SNAKE —even a little one. Nothing you do is right. Glide along in the only way you can, since you lack arms, legs, wings or fins, and you're sneaking up on something. Stop and you're preparing to strike. Raise your head off the ground so you can see better with those nearsighted eyes, and you're trying to throw a spell. Or sample the air with that incredibly delicate sense organ, your tongue, and—heavens!—you're flashing your stinger.

In fact, nothing you *don't* do is right, either. To grasp your tail in your mouth and roll downhill like a hoop is an idea in the realm of mythology, but you're still charged with such foolishness. It's the same with swallowing your babies for their protection, pilfering milk from defenseless cows in the barn, and poisoning people with that nonexistent dart in the end of your tail. But it's been this way since the first man peered out into the dark and imagined things. The unknown is somehow automatically to be feared.

This is how it is with the dozen or so species of snakes in Vermont. Almost every man's hand is against them. They're a full notch lower than a varmint, whatever that may be. And yet the truth about Vermont's

snakes is fully as amazing as the stories made up about them. And while the facts may never overcome childhood fears, they may succeed in presenting any snake for what it is: one of the most marvelously adapted creatures you'll ever meet.

Take their peculiar locomotion, for instance. If, as a child, you tried to squeeze in under some object such as a sofa, or maybe tried to negotiate Fat Man's Bend in a local rocky cave (as I did, and made it, too), you may have some idea of the handicap of no arms or legs. Under the sofa or in the narrow cave you were limited just to the use of your fingers and toes to shove you along. This, in effect, is just one of the problems that snakes have solved.

On rough or uneven ground a snake can take advantage of tiny projections, throwing its body into successive shallow loops and thus moving itself forward by forcing against these projections from the rear of each loop. In addition, each of the large under-scales, or scutes, overlaps the one behind it, with its free edge thus pointing backward. To glide, the snake reaches forward a tiny bit with each scute and presses backward, similar to the way you could inch along on your stomach by using your toes. With a hundred scutes or more work-

Far left is a smooth green snake, then, clockwise: a water snake, a garter snake,
a "dying" hognosed snake, a blacksnake, and below it a milk snake (checkered adder).

ing in harmony, the result is a steady glide.

This is fine for most purposes. But it is strictly one way: forward. Last summer I covered my blueberries with some old coarse-mesh netting to keep the birds away. A female grass, or garter, snake had poked an inquisitive nose into one of the squares of the net. Finding that it admitted her head, she continued forward. But what she hadn't reckoned on was that her black-and-yellow-striped body was not as lissome

as it had been earlier in the season. Carrying perhaps two dozen developing babies within her, she had that matronly air.

She crawled forward until she came to the beginning of the bulge where her future generation was stored. And there she stayed, held from backing out by the edge of the last scute which had been able to squeeze its way through the mesh.

When I discovered her, she'd apparently been a captive for a day or so, and was de-

177

cidedly weary of the whole affair. Seeing me, she renewed her struggles. Then, before my astonished eyes, she lightened her cargo by the simple process of giving birth to about fifteen babies. Her embarrassing corporation gone, she slipped the remainder of her body through the net. While I gaped, the entire company took off in sixteen different directions. Soon, no doubt, the incident would be forgotten, as the young searched for earthworms while the mother looked for frogs and toads. But the few unborn young she probably retained must have had quite a prenatal life before they were born in due course. Not only would they have been bumped along over the ground for a total of perhaps three months of unborn existence, but they would also have been almost throttled when their mother escaped through the blueberries' net.

It is this tendency to give birth when disturbed that probably produced the fiction that a mother snake swallows her babies. The young have a running start when born, so to speak, and can take care of themselves almost at once. Such precocious youngsters, therefore, *must* have fled back into their mother for protection: they simply couldn't have been newborn. And so the story also goes for the five harmless species of our snakes whose eggs hatch inside them, with the young remaining in the mother for a few days longer. These varieties would include the medium-sized garter, ribbon, and water snakes, plus the little brown and red-bellied snakes.

Of course the five Vermont snakes that lay eggs may never even see their own young. Hognosed, milk, black, green, and ring-necked snakes may abandon their eggs soon after they have deposited them. When the youngsters hatch from beneath their sun-warmed stone or from the little nest in the sand, they're on their own. No anxious mother hovers near to swallow them. But a good yarn dies hard.

Another myth illustrated by the floundering female concerns her tongue. It can do several things, but none of them is to sting. It is no more dangerous than an eyelash. In fact, an eyelash is a heavy club compared to the perfection of the snake's sensitive, two-pronged antenna.

Far from being strong enough to sting, the tongue of a snake is so delicate that its touch can scarcely be felt. My garter snake had no intention of threatening me with it. Rather, by sampling the air with its moist tissues, she was able to learn something about me. Picking up molecules in the air on her tongue, she'd transfer them to a special organ in the roof of her mouth. This exquisite chemical laboratory—known as Jacobson's organ, after its discoverer—would analyze my airborne trail. In addition to her normal sense of smell, it would tell her, far better than her brown eyes could judge, whether I was a living thing or merely a stone.

Had she actually touched me with her tongue, her information would have been increased enormously. Then she would have got what amounted to a taste. In fact, when I had a portly hognosed snake as a boy, I could sometimes trick it into eating cubes of meat instead of its preferred diet of toads by putting the meat in with a toad for a few hours. Although Chubby's eyes told him there was no toad there, his tongue couldn't lie: believing his tongue, he ate his square "toad" once a week.

The process by which a snake eats is like pulling a tight stocking over a foot. First one side, then the other, is worked forward. The jaws of a snake are equipped with loose hinges, somewhat like the slip-joint of a pair of pliers. They also have a flexible center cartilage between the right and left halves, top and bottom. Backward-

Blacksnake eggs hatching.

pointing teeth hook into the prey and the snake "walks" its way into its meal by alternately advancing right and left jaws.

Here too, a snake can move only forward. Once committed to a meal, it's bound to finish it. This is fine if it's only a snack, but if it amounts to a half-hour banquet, there's a new problem. The difficulty isn't the size of the meal, for a snake can stretch amazingly. But it also has to breathe.

The well-adapted snake is prepared for this eventuality, too. Near the base of the tongue is a tube which connects with the lungs. Thrust forward, the tube extends out into the air. The snake rests, takes a breather—then tucks its snorkel away and goes back to the work of swallowing.

After such a meal a snake may be logy for a week. Yet there is more to its life than just eating and keeping out of trouble. There's the matter of providing the world with more snakes, for instance. For all their reputation for cold-bloodedness, snakes show surprising solicitude in their lovemaking.

Most mating takes place in spring, soon after hibernation. It often occurs on a ledge or in a stone wall warmed by the sun, since a snake must absorb its temperature from its surroundings. Rubbing his nose along the body of the female and perhaps throwing a casual loop over her, the male caresses his intended with all the apparent concern of a boy taking his best girl to the drive-in. True to traditional girldom, the female acts as if she couldn't care less—at first. However, as the male's suit gains favor, she may rub and loop right back. Finally, when they are twined almost like the caduceus of a physician's insignia, mating takes place. Then, depending on the species and the climate, eggs are laid in soil nests in early summer. If it is a live-bearing species, the young are born in July and August.

One Monday morning at Vergennes high school a boy brought a satchel to our biology class. I had always encouraged my students to bring interesting specimens to school, so I was not surprised when I learned it contained a snake. "But not just *a* snake," Donald Codling confided. "There's thirty-two of 'em."

He had come across a group of garter

179

snakes, just out of hibernation, under a lumber pile, so we had an impromptu laboratory on snakes the rest of the week.

I jotted down comments of the students. Here are a few of them:

"I always thought they were wet and slimy. But they're dry and smooth. Not bad at all."

"Now I know why they don't blink their eyes. No eyelids."

"Yes, but they can move their eyes. See?"

"I guess 'cold-blooded' is the wrong term. This one was cold when I picked it off the lab table. Now it's just as warm as I am after I've held it and warmed it for a while."

"Can I take one home with me? I'll promise not to put it down anybody's neck on the bus."

Eventually fifteen snakes went home with new owners. And every one of the hundred and twenty-five students had touched a snake by Friday—urged on by curiosity and the promptings of their fellows. Hopefully, they all came to realize that a snake is, in reality, just another wild animal, and every bit as much a part of the outdoors as a mouse or a maple or a meadow lark.

Each of our Vermont species has its own interesting life history. The hognosed snake, or puffing adder—which ranges just barely into southern Vermont all the way from the Gulf Coast—is too stocky to escape many enemies. Instead, it has developed a unique means of defense. Flattening out to twice its normal size, it hisses and strikes at any offending creature. At this point the offending creature usually looks for a stick, if a human being, or backs away respectfully if not.

However, if the sham doesn't work and the intruder accidentally notices that the snake's "vicious strike" is often made (surprisingly) with jaws closed, the puff adder goes into Phase Two of its little drama.

Suddenly seized with what appears to be the terminal stage of apoplexy, it rolls about in a frenzy. Its jaw drops open, its tongue hangs out, and it rolls over onto its back—dead.

If the enemy picks the snake up, it hangs limp as a dead snake should. But then if it's turned over on its belly, the "dead" snake goes into Phase Three. This consists of rolling smartly over onto its back again. Apparently, as the great herpetologist Raymond Ditmars once remarked, the idea is that the only position for a dead snake is on its back.

Other snakes in the Green Mountains have their personalities, too. There's the common milk snake—also known as the checkered adder—which has been saddled with the delightful tale that it steals milk from cows as they stand meekly in the barn. In reality no self-respecting bovine would put up with such nonsense.

Actually the milk snake comes in from the fields and brushland on a more commendable errand: to perform as a mousetrap. Able to follow rats and mice right into their holes and devour the young, it can do the job better than any cat.

If the three-foot-long milk snake is able to do such good work on rodents, its larger cousin, the blacksnake or racer, should be that much better. One of the unforgettable sights of my youth was watching a five-foot blacksnake enter a mousehole at the edge of a meadow. It got results in ten seconds. To the accompaniment of squeaks of alarm, mice erupted in all directions from holes I never knew existed. They leaped out, dived back in another hole, and leaped out again. That portion of the meadow looked like a field of strange, brown popping corn.

Both these snakes sometimes get carried away in their crusades, however. A milk snake was the downfall of a nest of tree swallows in a birdhouse six feet from the

The shy, mild-tempered rattler—almost never seen in Vermont.

ground at my home in Lincoln. And one time I arrived at a friend's home just in time to rescue three baby catbirds in a rosebush from a sixty-five-inch blacksnake. But, as my friend charitably pointed out, "I can't blame him too much. After all, catbirds have been doing fine for thousands of years before we came along to save them from the blacksnake."

Vermont has a number of small-sized snakes too: the red-bellied, ring-necked, and the brown varieties found under logs and stones. They feed on insects and other small creatures that share their territory, and aren't much bigger than a good-sized earthworm. As one fifth-grader told me, presenting a twelve-inch red-bellied snake: "You can have it, Mr. Rood. It ain't even big enough to scare girls with."

Sometimes we come across the smooth green snake at the edge of a meadow, or the yellow-striped ribbon snake along a streambank. The former, about two feet in length, and the latter a little longer, are "big enough to scare girls," but they don't get the chance very often. Both slender species are too well camouflaged to be noticed. As

they glide through the grass in search of insects, spiders and amphibians, they seem to melt into their surroundings. They are so graceful and smooth in their movements that more than once I've stared at what I thought was a stationary snake only to have it grow thinner before my eyes, suddenly turn into a tail tip, and then disappear.

The vanishing trick is a specialty of the water snake, too. One of the shyest species, it drops into the water from its basking log before you can drift close. Like most snakes its body is very sensitive to vibrations, so even if it happens to be facing the other way, it can feel the impact of ripples from an approaching boat. A few flicks of its tongue to sample the air for odors and more vibrations—and it dives to the bottom.

For its diet of fish and frogs the water snake often chooses the slower species, leaving the swifter simply because it cannot catch them. Of course it is not a water moccasin, but its four-foot body, as thick as your wrist, makes people think it must be. The real moccasin, or cottonmouth, doesn't get anywhere near this far north.

181

The little-seen timber rattlesnake puts on the best disappearing act of them all. It can produce a wonderful optical illusion of being there when it's nowhere around. You don't need to be more than a year or two in Vermont before you begin to hear of rattlesnakes. They are always gigantic in size, always discovered about to attack an unwary vacationist or innocent child—and always neatly disposed of where they can't be found again when you go to see for yourself.

The rattler sometimes gets credit for the antics of other snakes, too. Black, garter, and milk snakes will vibrate the tail when disturbed; if this happens to take place in dry leaves, there's the sound of your rattlesnake. The milk snake's checkered body, of course, makes it a "rattlesnake" for sure.

Actually, the range of the rattler does extend as far north as the southern half of Vermont, where it is still found in a few rugged ledges and rocky wastelands. Shy, retiring and mild-tempered, though, it is seldom seen even in places where it's known to exist. Accidental bites are so rare that many doctors have never seen a case. Yet one member of the Vermont Camping Association winced when I told him I was writing about the state's snakes. "We'll probably get a dozen cancellations," he said; "it happens every time someone mentions the word 'rattlesnake.' People want to get out-of-doors, but they don't want to get down to earth."

The cause of all this misplaced apprehension is a creature of unusual gifts. Not only does the rattler have the ability to "smell" with its tongue and "hear" with its body as do the ten other Vermont species, but it carries a delicate heat detector as well. This is in the form of a pit between the eye and nostril, and larger than the nostril itself. Delicate nerves in the pit are amazingly sensitive to slight heat changes.

When a warm-blooded animal, such as a rodent or small bird, has been struck by a rattlesnake, the snake retires until its victim has ceased thrashing around. Then, guided largely by its heat detector, it "homes in" on its prey. The U. S. Air Force's Sidewinder missile is so named because it uses a heat-detector system to find its target, too.

The possessor of these talents averages something over three feet long. It is dressed in a pattern allowing it to lie unnoticed among the leaves: yellow with brown or black crossbands, or entirely dark in color. The newborn young are attractive, with their banded bodies, but they've got snippy dispositions. They will defend themselves with tiny poison fangs that can give a painful wound. They also shake their single little button on the end of their tails, but it is firmly attached and won't rattle.

With maturity, the snippy disposition calms down. The rattle develops loose segments as the skin is shed, sometimes two or three times a year. Like that of other snakes, the outer skin is rubbed off on a rough object, usually starting at the chin. The reptile crawls out of it, turning it inside out in the process. Generally the skin is stretched, too—which doubtless accounts for not a few stories of monster snakes which forever threaten our very existence. I have a tattered eight-foot blacksnake skin from Monkton, for instance—nearly two feet longer than the maximum size for the species, and probably three feet longer than its actual owner. It was brought to me by a wide-eyed boy who was all for getting up a posse to track it to its lair and slay it.

All of which, as I said, makes it tough to be a snake, even a little one. And to make it worse, for many people there *are* no little snakes.

The Authors and Illustrators

In 1939 Jonathan Daniels wrote, "There's a poet under the politician in Governor Aiken of Vermont; he wrote some of it in the preface to his *Pioneering with Wildflowers.*" The Hon. GEORGE D. AIKEN of Putney, U. S. Senator since 1940, still lists himself as "farmer," and his interest in nature and conservation and his detailed knowledge of state affairs continue despite heavy national and international concerns. Senator Aiken's family have been Vermonters since before the Revolution, and no public figure in this century has so well spoken for Vermonters of all political hues, or so well typified Vermont attitudes.

PHILIP F. ALLAN, senior biologist of the Soil Conservation Service, has been with that agency for more than thirty years. A New Hampshire native, he now lives in Upper Darby, Pennsylvania.

HAL BORLAND of Salisbury, Connecticut, one of the nation's leading nature and conservation writers, has lived in the East since 1926. In addition to numerous magazine articles he has published twenty-four books as novelist, poet, and essayist. In 1967 he received the Edward J. Meeman Conservation Award.

Zoological work and collecting after World War II led the late EDWARD J. BRUNDAGE to study and then to drawing botanical and forestry subjects. A group of conservationists has acquired a rare collection of his bird paintings.

SONJA BULLATY and ANGELO LOMEO of New York City, a husband-and-wife team whose work appears regularly in mass-circulation magazines, are internationally known for their black-and-white and color photographs of art, nature and people of North and Central America, eastern Europe, the Near East, and Africa. Long-time Vermont enthusiasts, they have been doing photographic assignments for *Vermont Life* since 1955.

ROBERT CANDY, a freelance illustrator of national repute, is public information officer for the Vermont Fish and Game Service. His nature illustrations have appeared in many magazines and in trade and textbooks. He has both written and illustrated a number of books, including *Nature Notebook* and *Big Jack.* He and his family now make their home in Montpelier.

HANSON CARROLL, the photographer most represented in *Vermont Life* over the years, lives with his wife and two sons in Norwich. His interests are reflected in the front-cover photograph, and in work appearing in *Sports Illustrated, True,* and other national magazines.

The late MIRIAM CHAPIN spent her childhood in Pittsford, and graduated from the University of Vermont, majoring in botany. She moved in 1934 to Montreal, where she was correspondent for the *Christian Science Monitor* and wrote for American magazines. Her books include *How People Talk, Quebec Now* and *Contemporary Canada.*

Illustrator GEORGE DALY came to Vermont in 1940 to do art and advertising work. From then until 1959, when he and his family moved to Washington State, he served in the U. S. Air Force and later freelanced with book, magazine and advertising art. He now concentrates on airplane design, with occasional illustrating.

LEON W. DEAN of Burlington, until his retirement a professor of English at the University of Vermont, is the author of many articles and books for young people, and has long been a prime mover in the Vermont Folklore Society.

RICHARD R. FRUTCHEY, who took the photograph on the back cover, lives in Cranford, New Jersey.

ERNEST GAY is an author-photographer specializing in nature and sports. A native of Hawaii, he moved in 1964 to South Newfane with his family.

WALTER R. HARD, JR., a Vermont native and now Burlington resident, has been editor in chief of *Vermont Life* since 1950, and is author of *The Vermont Guide*.

HAROLD B. HITCHCOCK heads the biology department at Middlebury College, where he joined the faculty in 1943. His interest in bats continues.

Photographer and nature writer CHARLES CLEVELAND JOHNSON, a New York resident, had broad experience in technical and aerial photography before his interest in natural history became dominant. Most of his time since 1962 has been spent filming for the New York Botanical Garden's vast publishing effort, *Wildflowers of the United States*. Prior to that he collaborated on illustrations for *Wildflowers of North America*.

CLEMENS KALISCHER of Stockbridge, Massachusetts, is a photographer in many fields who has an international reputation for his work in black and white. He films extensively in Vermont.

Designer FRANK LIEBERMAN (*Vermont Life*'s art director since 1963) studied in New York, Munich and Vienna, did design work in London, and since 1959 has been freelancing for magazine and book publishers from his home in Woodstock. Among his many interests are mycology and cooking.

BENJAMIN E. ROGERS has for some years had his own photography studio in Middlebury.

RONALD ROOD's love of nature and the wild began in his Connecticut boyhood. He received his B.S. and later his M.S. in wildlife management from the University of Connecticut, and between times served as a fighter pilot in Europe. With his wife, Peg, and their four children, he moved in 1953 to Lincoln. Now a full-time author and lecturer, he is a regular contributor to national magazines, has written six natural history books for children, and two of his earlier adult titles have been chosen by the Natural Science Book Club. His very popular series of articles on wildlife began in *Vermont Life* in 1960.

The trout illustration by WILLIAM J. SCHALDACH appeared in a 1947 issue of *Vermont Life* while the famed nature illustrator was still living in central Vermont.

JOHN F. SMITH, JR., who heads the Audio-Visual department at the University of Vermont, has been an active professional photographer since his graduation from Middlebury College.

MILFORD K. SMITH of Rutland, who is an Associate Justice of the Vermont Supreme Court, since boyhood had been immersed in outdoor Vermont, particularly Indian archeology, hunting and fishing, with special emphasis on trout. His weekly outdoor column has appeared for many years in the *Rutland Daily Herald*.

The noted American nature writer EDWIN WAY TEALE, whose home is in Connecticut, has been a freelance author of books on natural history since 1941. Most famous are his four books of the American Seasons Series of the twenty-five he has written and edited. His article on the gulls of Champlain was written for *Vermont Life* in 1964.

HAROLD C. TODD's scenes of nature appeared frequently in *Vermont Life* during the 1950's when he was a frequent visitor to Peru. His home is in Fanwood, New Jersey.

Index

185

The text of this book has been set in Baskerville type, and the headings in Times Roman, by Vermont Printing Company of Brattleboro, Vermont. The text has been printed by lithography, and the color plates by letterpress, at the Rumford Press, Concord, New Hampshire. The binding has been done by the Book Press of Brattleboro. The book was designed by R. L. Dothard Associates.

188